P9-CQZ-150

JUST
A GUY

JUST
A GUY

Notes from a Blue Collar Life

BILL ENGVALL

with **ALAN EISENSTOCK**

ST. MARTIN'S PRESS
NEW YORK

www.stmartins.com

Designed by Dylan R. Greif

ISBN-13: 978-0-312-36267-6
ISBN-10: 0-312-36267-6

First Edition: June 2007

10 9 8 7 6 5 4 3 2 1

Bill:
To Gail, Emily, and Travis.
Without you there is no life.

Alan:
To the A Team: B, J, K, and Z.

CONTENTS

Acknowledgments ....*xi*

1. EATING, SLEEPING, AND SEX........................*1*

2. LIKE A HURRICANE....................................*6*

3. ER...*9*

4. THE MONSTER UNDER THE BED.................*12*

5. BILL'S DEAD...*18*

6. OUT OF THE CLOSET................................*21*

7. SIX ICE TEAS..*28*

8. BIG FISH..*31*

9. TEARS OF A CLOWN.................................*36*

10. HOT DOG BUBBLE GUM..........................*38*

11. THE BEST DAY OF MY LIFE......................*45*

12. THE WORST DAY OF MY LIFE...................*48*

13. CLEMENTINE..*52*

More
CONTENTS

14. TURKEY SHOOT...............................58

15. HORMONES ON THE RANGE.......................62

16. I FOUGHT THE LAW...........................66

17. MARRYING MISS MILLER...........................70

18. GOOD 'N' GREASY...........................74

19. GOING TO THE DRIVE-IN...........................80

20. LEAVING ARIZONA...........................85

21. THE DEATH OF COOL...........................88

22. I SHOT THE SHERIFF 93

23. THE THIRTY-MINUTE RULE...........................98

24. COLLEGE DAZE...........................105

25. BURNING DOWN THE HOUSE...................109

26. TEQUILA AND LONGNECKS 114

27. CAVE MAN...........................120

Even More
CONTENTS

28. I WRITE THE SONGS 126

29. RIP CORD 131

30. ROLLER DERBY QUEEN 136

31. EMIL FROM THE KITCHEN 139

32. IT HAPPENED ONE NIGHT 145

33. DEMON LOVER 154

34. BUDDY, BUDDY 159

35. POPPING THE QUESTION 163

36. THE JELLYFISH STUNG ME
    ON MY PEE-PEE 167

37. TEXAS BIG HAIR 175

38. SCREAM 185

39. QUALITY TIME 190

40. BLOOD SIMPLE 195

Contents, Contents,
CONTENTS

41. JUST A MAN *200*

42. BRA SHOPPING *209*

43. CRAPPY PARENT *213*

44. HITTING THE CURVE *217*

45. SEÑOR A-HOLAY *228*

46. THE INVISIBLE MAN *234*

ACKNOWLEDGMENTS

BILL: Bill and Mary Engvall, Jeanne and Neal McCormick, Janet McTigue, Judy Collins, and Rick and Jenny Jackson. To everyone in my extended family, thank you. A special acknowledgment to JP Williams. You are, in a word, AMAZING!!! Maggie Houlehan—because of your tireless work and friendship I am forever in debt. Bud and Dorise Watson, Ben Sevier, the great staff at Vigliano and Associates, everyone at St. Martin's Press, and all those people who have been involved in my career; there are too many of you to name. My most heartfelt thanks to all of you who have crossed my path. You have in no small way shaped my life. A special thank you to Alan Eisenstock. Thanks for listening to me drone on about my life and still making me sound interesting.

ALAN: Thanks, Bill, thanks, Gail. It was a blast.

Huge thanks to David Vigliano and all his Associates, fabulous editor Ben Sevier, Elizabeth Beier, Jen Crawford, India Cooper, and everyone at St. Martin's Press, David Ritz, Shirley and Jim Eisenstock, Madeline and Phil Schwarzman, Susan Pomerantz and George Weinberger, Susan Baskin and Richard Gerwitz, Edwin Greenberg and Elaine Gordon, Linda Nussbaum, Randy Turtle, Randy Feldman, Loretta, Brian, Linda, Lorraine, Diane, Alan, Ben, Chris, and Nathan, Diane Golden, Judi Farkas, Bob Vickrey, Katie O'Laughlin, and Connie, Mia, Danielle, Ed, Andrea, Jessica, Barbara, and Amy at Village Books in Pacific Palisades, California, my reading room.

A nod to Rhett Miller and the Old 97s, who made me hear it and feel it.

Special thanks to Bobbie, who still laughs out loud at the good parts.

JUST
A GUY

1. EATING, SLEEPING, AND SEX

Welcome to the story of my life.

Let's start with the basics.

Like who am I?

Oh, I know you know that I'm the comedian who came up with "Here's Your Sign" and that I'm a member of the cast of the Blue Collar Comedy Tour and Blue Collar TV. I'm the one who's not Jeff, Ron, or Larry the Cable Guy. Yeah. That one. That's me.

But who am I really?

That's what I'm about to tell you. I'm a little nervous because I know what's coming. I'm about to reveal some stuff that's very personal, a little bit embarrassing, and sometimes kind of strange. I think there's a decent chance you'll chuckle once or twice. You might even tear up. Hopefully not at the same time.

Now, a couple things you should know about me before we get started.

First, I'm unbelievably normal. Unlike many comedians and serial killers, which my dad considers the same thing, I don't come from a screwed-up, crazy family. I was never smacked around, molested, or locked in a fruit cellar. Sorry. I'm pretty much the boy next door, the kid riding his bike down the street, the guy on the other side of the classroom. Okay, I'm the one with the chalk up my nose, but only because the teacher's putting me to sleep and I'm trying to amuse myself until the bell rings. So that's me. You know me well. You've hung out with me after school, gone to the movies with me, played ball against me—and if you're a girl, you've probably ignored me.

The second thing you need to know is that I'm a guy. Been one my whole life, which makes me an expert on the subject. As my wife, Gail, says, "You've been doing research for almost fifty years." True. My lab is my life.

So let me clear something up right here. This might shake your world if you're a woman, but I can't help it. This is an indisputable scientific fact:

All guys are the same.

Doesn't matter if you teach college or drive a forklift. A guy is a guy. Nothing we can do about it. Now, in case you're not a guy, here's the dictionary definition:

A person who doesn't think before he speaks.

We just don't. We can't. Our brains are not wired to think. The truth is we're not that deep.

A guy has only three basic needs: eating, sleeping, and sex. That's it. That's our whole day. I know a lot of women don't believe it, but it's true. If you see a guy thinking really hard, chances are two of his basic needs have been met and he's trying to figure out how to take care of number three.

"I ate, I slept . . . where can I get me some sex?"

The one thing we've got going for us is that we have an excuse when we do something dumb. If Gail catches me doing something lame, which has happened occasionally in the twenty-four years of our marriage, I'll just look at her and shrug.

"Sorry, honey, I'm just a *guy*."

Part of being a guy is that I don't care about the same things my wife does. Like balancing the checkbook. She reconciles it every month, and if it's off by one penny, she'll get out the calculator and go through the check register until she finds it. With me, if it's within a hundred bucks, cool, it's balanced. Next problem.

Sometimes being a guy makes us vulnerable. For one thing, the marketing people are on to us. They know we're guys, and they take advantage of us. It ticks me off. I know there's nothing I can do about it, but I try to fight my little battles by letting them know that I know what they're doing.

Like taking advantage of how we smell.

Let me ask a profound question.

What is the difference between cologne and aftershave? Take a moment.

Give up? I'll tell you.

There is no freaking difference.

Same stuff, different bottle. It's just marketing. It's like the difference between a comb and a brush. Which is? Not that much. They both do the same thing: move your hair from front to back, back to front, and back again.

What's amazing is that somehow we've been duped into buying both cologne and aftershave. Because as a group, guys just ain't that particular about grooming. My day is not ruined if I don't get a shower right off the bat. I can work out, come back, and shower later. Gail doesn't get this.

"How can you not shower? You just worked out."

"Well, yeah, but the sweat's dry."

I don't need to shower to go out to lunch. I'll just throw a ball cap on and go. Gail cannot be that spontaneous. If I say, "Hey, let's go out for lunch," she's lost.

"Now? I haven't done my hair."

"Put a ball cap on. Let's go."

"I can't—"

"You look great. Come *on*."

Naw, it ain't happening. It just can't. The first clue is inside the medicine cabinet. Just check out the difference between a woman's medicine cabinet and a guy's. I've got shaving cream, my razor, toothpaste, and cologne. That's it. Gail's got facial washes, powders, makeup, creams, hair sprays, mousses, gels, and body lotions. CVS has less stuff. It's astonishing. She always looks good and smells good, and I swear it's natural. To me, she doesn't need anything added to go out. But she feels she's gotta do a makeover to go out and get a sandwich.

The way Madison Avenue gets to us is to market stuff that makes us think we'll get sex. For instance:

There's this new body spray. You've seen the commercials. A guy sprays this stuff on and suddenly he's got dozens of girls climbing all over him. Yeah, right, I believe *that*.

I bought some.

On the off chance that the stuff works.

I sprayed it on and walked into the kitchen, where Gail was balancing the checkbook, agonizing over fourteen cents she couldn't find. She looked up, sniffed the air, and made a face like I'd dragged in a dead animal.

"Something smells."

"It could be my new body spray."

"Body spray?"

"Yeah," I said, edging closer to her. "It's supposed to make me hot to you."

She fanned her nose trying to kill the smell. "You're stinking up the kitchen. And get away from me. *Whoo*."

Not exactly the result I was hoping for.

But it does prove that guys will try anything to take care of our three basic needs. Actually, as you'll see, lathering myself up with body spray is mild compared to most of the stuff I've done in my life.

So sit back, relax, put your feet up, and come along for the read.

2. LIKE A HURRICANE

According to my parents, grandparents, and close family friends, I was born in Galveston, Texas, on July 27, 1957, right in the middle of Hurricane Audrey.

According to everything I've ever read, Hurricane Audrey hit Galveston on *June* 27, 1957. So either all those people were drinking heavily or my birth lasted a month. Or, as I actually believe, my entrance into the world came on like a hurricane.

My father was a medical student at the time, doing his internship in the hospital in Galveston. We lived nearby in LaMarque, Texas, a tiny town known primarily for dust. I don't recall much else about LaMarque because Dad moved Mom and me to Baltimore shortly after I was born. By then he'd finished medical school and gone into the government health service.

My dad cut a striking figure: a doctor in a uniform. A couple of old pictures I found show him holding me, a chunky butterball, shirtless, grinning like the Gerber baby, while Dad's smiling widely in his Navy uniform. Instead of a cluster of medals on his pocket, he wears a large clump of dried milk and drool stains. His smile said he didn't mind.

In Baltimore we lived in government housing, a line of brownstones, or row houses, all of which were identical. The government paid our rent, so you know this was the cheapest housing they could find. Of course, today that neighborhood is gentrified and those brownstones probably go for a bazillion apiece. Back then you were lucky if you could tell which house was yours, something I could do with ease even though I couldn't read yet, a feat my grandfather found amazing.

I loved when my grandparents visited. They spoiled me like crazy. When my sister Janet came along, they visited even more and paid as much attention to me as to her. Can't blame 'em. There wasn't much you could do with her. She was just a howling baby with no personality, just a lot of demands. At least I had a sense of humor.

Yep. Early on, by age two, I started to show signs that at any given moment, I would always go for the joke.

My grandfather swore this story is true, but I don't remember it. I'll take his word because it sounds like me.

It was a sunny afternoon, and Granddad had taken me for a walk. He was holding me, and we were strolling down the street outside our row house. He stopped to talk to one of our neighbors, a very proper, well-dressed woman around his age. He started patting me gently on the back as they talked. All of a sudden I let out some very loud gas, what I later referred to when I had kids as a butt burp.

"Granpa!" I said, and I grabbed his face and shook my head.

He broke up. The woman didn't. Either she thought he was the culprit, or she didn't think it was funny for me to blame my grandfather, because she stormed off.

Oh well. Some people just don't appreciate a good fart joke.

3. ER

I was never a wild or crazy kid, but for some reason I seemed to spend an enormous amount of time in the emergency room. Some people might say I was accident-prone, others that I was just a typical boy. A few people called me by the accepted medical term: klutz.

After Janet was born, the government decided that we'd had enough fun time in Baltimore and moved us back to Galveston. Dad found a small house on a cul-de-sac where the street was made of oyster shells. I couldn't believe my good luck. A street made of actual *oyster shells?*

Do you know what an oyster shell sounds like

when you throw it? It makes a low-pitched whirring sound, a cross between a guitar plunk and a kazoo. If you zing an oyster shell just right, you can turn it into a singing martial arts weapon, which is what my friends and I used to do. We'd play army and sidearm the shells at each other. Incredibly cool. Until a shell sliced you across the face and sent you to the ER for stitches—for me, a weekly occurrence. I have several "oyster-chuck" scars on my face, souvenirs of Galveston.

The other bonus of living in Galveston was that the streets in our neighborhood were blessed with ditches on either side. These filled up with water when it rained and then luckily became infested with crawfish. Also great martial arts weapons. We would pluck the crawfish out of the mud and hurl them at each other, all in one motion. If you were really good and really lucky, you could get a crawfish to land on your buddy, dig its claws into his skin, and hang on. So cool. Got a couple of excellent crawfish scars on me, too.

My favorite toy to play with in Galveston was the garden hose. In almost every picture I'm in you can see me standing on the lawn, shirtless, a little bit tubby, grinning goofily, the garden hose in my hand. I'm not sure if there is any symbolism there. We'll let future Blue Collar scholars and shrinks sort that out. Let's just say I was very attached to my hose.

One day, my sister Janet decided that she had just as much right to that hose as I did.

She was wrong. It was my hose. You do not mess with another gardener's equipment.

I found her standing on the lawn, swinging my hose around her head, trying to make weird water patterns or create a rainbow effect or some such nonsense.

No. It was *my* hose.

I told Janet to put it down. She ignored me and kept swinging the hose around her head. I asked her one last time to put down my hose. She turned her back on me, pretending she didn't hear me.

I charged her. She whirled around. What I didn't realize was that the hose had a jagged sprinkler attached to the end. I ran right into it, face first. I saw stars and heard birds chirping, and the next thing you know I was heading for the emergency room and seven more stitches. The ER should have given me one of those cards where after ten visits you get the eleventh one free.

Then there was one time that I avoided landing in the emergency room because I was almost killed.

For my birthday, my parents gave me a red plastic train engine that I pedaled around everywhere. I rode in that train so much that I actually gave up the garden hose. I drove my train inside the house, down the driveway, and up and down the sidewalk.

One day I decided to go on a road trip. Literally. I pedaled out into the street. Didn't see the car coming. The car screeched to a stop a foot away from me. My mother screamed, I screamed, and the driver of the car screamed.

I'm sorry, but I had the right-of-way.

Everybody knows that a car is supposed to stop for a train.

4. THE MONSTER UNDER THE BED

Next stop, Jasper, Texas, where my second sister, Judy, was born. In Jasper, we lived in a rambling, ranch-style house with a huge backyard dotted with pine trees. In the far corner of the yard, half hidden by the trees, was a small shed that served many purposes for my vivid imagination. I'd graduated from playing with the garden hose and pedaling my train to inventing fantasy games in the yard, sometimes with friends, sometimes alone. That shed became a medieval castle, an outlaw's hideout, a World War II prison, a Mars outpost. I would run through the fallen pinecones, the scent of evergreen at my back, pretending that I was Underdog or Speed Racer or some other superhero I'd created. In every story I made up, I faced insurmountable odds and superhuman foes, all of which I destroyed by the end of each afternoon.

Except one time.

It was a hot summer afternoon. I flew across the yard in pursuit of a hideous imaginary villain. I raced around the side of the shed and came face-to-face with two enormous, coiled green snakes. They seemed to raise themselves to a height of ten feet, then hissed simultaneously and opened their mouths wide as alligators. They lunged forward, attempting to swallow me whole.

I spun around and sprinted toward the house. I'd never seen a live snake before. Excuse me. *Twin* live snakes. I'd seen pictures, but in the pictures the snakes had not hissed, coiled, lunged, and tried to have me for lunch. As I ran, sweat and tears streamed down my face. I tore up the walk and almost ran right through our screen door. I never looked back, but I *know* those snakes were slithering right behind me, nipping at my heels. I raced into the kitchen and dove under the table, got into a fetal position, and stayed there for something like a week.

To this day, I am deathly afraid of snakes. No wonder in the Bible a snake is cast as the devil. For one thing, they move without legs. That's not natural.

Pure evil. That's what they are.

A short time later my youngest sister, Jenny, came along. That made the score in our family three girls to one boy. Talk about unfair odds. My sisters had no chance against me.

As a typically obnoxious older brother, I woke up every morning with one goal: to think up new and diabolical ways to torture my sisters. Especially Janet. That was my mission.

I did have certain rules to make it interesting. For example, if I wanted to gross one of my sisters out, I couldn't just say something mildly disgusting and move on. No. I had to gross her out so much that she'd run screaming from the room. If I wanted to make her laugh, I had to get her laughing so hard that whatever she was drinking would come pouring out of her nose. And if I wanted to scare her, always my favorite, I had to scare her so much that she ran out of the room shrieking and crying *and* begging to go sleep with our parents.

Grossing out Janet was easy. I'd just recount in gory detail my latest adventure in the emergency room, sprinkling in my own personal touch to seal the deal:

"My head was bleeding. Blood was gushing out of both of my ears, like faucets. I heard them say they had to operate. But they didn't give me enough anesthetic. I was totally awake. I could see everything. I tried to speak, but they'd jammed a plastic mask over my mouth. Then the doctor came in. He was really old, and I think he was blind because he came in tapping the floor with a cane. He went over to the wrong patient. The nurse turned him around and led him over to me. He picked up a scalpel. His hand was shaking. It was like he had palsy or something. Then he made the incision . . . and he missed! This old blind palsy doctor accidentally cut off my right nipple! Did you hear me? *He cut off my nipple!* I'm deformed! I'm hideous! Do you want to see my empty nipple socket?"

"Noooo!!! Ahhhh! Groooosss!" And she'd run screaming out of the room.

Score!

Making all my sisters laugh wasn't even a challenge. They were younger than me and easy targets. Pretty much all I had to do was an impression of one of my parents or grandparents. All parents have a habit of repeating themselves over and over. I'd just do that until my sisters would start laughing. Again, the key was to wait until they were eating or drinking. Somehow you laugh more when you've try-ing to chew or swallow. Makes it so worth the wait.

The hardest goal to achieve was scaring them. Since there were three of them, they automatically had safety in numbers. After I'd suc-ceeded in scaring them once by waiting in the closet and then jump-ing out when Judy opened the door, they were always on alert. As in all things, in particular torturing your siblings, the essential element is patience. You must be willing to bide your time.

My favorite tactic was to slide under the bed while one of them was in the bathroom. Sometimes I'd stay hidden under there for an hour, just waiting for the perfect moment. As soon as my oblivious sis-ter would come into the room and step next to the bed, I'd reach out, grab her ankle, and pull.

A word of advice. It's always tempting to add a low growl or a high-pitched laugh, but don't. Much better to grab silently, without warning. That way, with some luck and the right timing, you might get your sister to totally flip out. You want to get her to scream loud enough to rattle the windows.

If two of my sisters happened to come in together, I'd reach out and grab both at the same time. That didn't happen often, but when it did, my day was made.

Unfortunately, my last memory of living in Jasper is not a happy one. In some sense, I guess I got repaid for all the horror I inflicted on my sisters.

The three of them shared a room. Their beds were lined up, side by side. One of our favorite games was bed jumping. We would jump from bed to bed to bed, incorporating various moves, leaps, and dives. One night, Mom and Dad decided to go out together, just the two of them. They hired a babysitter, a kindly older woman who took care of us by planting herself in front of the television set and nursing an ice tea. I guess her babysitting philosophy was "I'll tune in the TV and tune them out."

Before they left, my father turned to us, to me in particular, and said, "While we're gone, do not, I repeat, do *not* jump on the beds. You got that?"

"Sure, Dad," I said, and my sisters nodded enthusiastically.

We waited until the babysitter set up camp in front of the TV, then we closed the bedroom door and started bed jumping.

I have to say, in all modesty, that I was by far the world's best bed jumper. I combined a natural flair for style with a sheer gift for distance. This night I was determined to break the all-time bed-jumping distance record, set a couple of nights before by, you guessed it, me.

We began in our usual way, by warming up. The three of us hopped from bed to bed, casually, getting our timing down, preparing for the big jump. When the time was right, everyone got out of my way.

There are moments in sports, special moments, that we, as a nation, have been privileged to witness: the U.S. Olympic hockey team defeating the Russians; Michael Jordan single-handedly clinching his final NBA title; Barry Bonds amassing his home-run records.

Those moments pale compared to the night that I broke the all-time bed-jumping record.

I could tell the old record was history the second I launched myself from the first bed. I just knew. My altitude was breathtakingly high, my form astonishingly perfect. I felt myself arching in the air, taking flight toward a record that would never be broken.

There was only one factor I had not considered.

During our warm-ups, the third bed had been pushed several feet from its original position. Consequently, I greatly miscalculated my necessary trajectory.

In other words, I missed the bed.

My foot came down on the metal bed frame. In slow motion, I saw my foot split open from heel to toe. A fountain of blood spurted out. We're talking about a geyser of blood. There was more blood in that bedroom than in all of the *Saw* movies put together.

My sisters screamed and ran to the babysitter, who hoisted herself off the couch and called my parents at the restaurant, resulting in yet another visit to the ER, where I received yet another row of stitches on yet another body part.

But there was a silver lining.

I truly grossed out my sisters.

5. BILL'S DEAD

Around this time, my dad left the government health service and went into private practice. He found a great position in Winslow, Arizona, where he moved us. I spent my formative years in Winslow, most of elementary school and all of junior high, and to this day, I think of Winslow as home. I loved growing up there. I even grew out of having an accident a minute, except for one last, dramatic incident.

Even when I was in elementary school, I was just a guy, which is always the main point you have to remember about me. Then and now, I don't think things through. I live by my wit and my instinct, a truly stupid way to live.

I was in the fourth grade, and my buddy and I were riding our bikes in the playground. I had just gotten a new bike, a Sting-Ray, and I was feeling way cool. My pal and I had gotten into a rhythm of riding in and out of the chin-up bars. Out of the corner of my eye, I noticed that two extremely cute older women, fifth graders, were checking us out. They were trying to act nonchalant, but by the way they were giggling, it was obvious they were into us.

Being cool and a guy, I knew that riding in and out of the chin-up bars, doing a wheelie here and a three-sixty turn with a skid there, wasn't enough. Wasn't enough for what, I had no idea. I just knew that I had to do more.

I decided to go for something special, an Evel Knievel stunt. My plan was simple, yet thrillingly extreme. I would back up fifty yards, burn rubber, and ride as fast as I could toward the chin-up bars. As soon as I got close, I'd grab hold of a bar, let go of the bike, and swing, suspended in midair like Tarzan. The girls would be impressed. The girls would be *mine*.

I got into position. I pushed off and started pedaling furiously toward the chin-up bars. What I did not take into consideration was that it was drizzling steadily and that the metal chin-up bars were wet and slippery. I arrived at the chin-up bars, grabbed hold, let go of the bike, pulled myself up, and—

My hands slipped. I tumbled downward and hit the pavement head first.

That's the last thing I remember.

The girls screamed and, I was told later, held on to each other for emotional support. My buddy hopped onto his bike and rode over to our house, which fortunately was right across the street. Unfortunately, my mom was in bed with the flu. My buddy burst into our house and shouted, "Bill's dead!"

My mother threw off her bedclothes and ran toward the playground. By this time, I had regained consciousness. Through my snowy, blurred vision I saw my mom, in her nightgown, running toward me as I lay spread out on the asphalt.

"Bill!" she screamed.

I'm not dead, I thought, but as my mom, in her flimsy rain-soaked night gown, leaned over me, and I saw the girls doubled over with laughter and pointing at us, I said aloud, "But I wish I was."

6. OUT OF THE CLOSET

In reality, I'm sure that Winslow was a town like a thousand others, sleepy, nondescript, and unremarkable, but in my mind, Winslow is a kind of dreamland, a piece of Americana that may only exist in my memory and in my imagination.

I remember Winslow as a series of interconnecting grids at the edge of the desert. Our downtown consisted of a few blocks of stores, a city hall, a post office, and a movie theater. We had every type of store we needed, and the store clerks knew every customer by name. I remember warm days, cool nights, the scent of desert flowers, and my lungs filling up with crisp, clear air as I ran to first base or rode my bike down the street. Winslow was a community of honest, hardworking people who looked out for each other and treated strangers as family. I could walk anywhere, day or night, without fear. We never locked our doors, and we always invited everyone in.

Of course, it was a different world then, a simpler world, a slower world, before cell phones, video games, and computers. There was no such thing as identity theft because everybody knew who you were. I'm not one to glorify the "good old days," but in some ways I think they were better. These days, my sixteen-year-old son never leaves his room. All of his entertainment comes to him through iTunes, his Xbox, or DVDs and downloads on his iMac. I never enjoyed any entertainment in my room. I had a bed, a desk, and a ViewMaster. Clicking the same twelve slides of Bugs Bunny and Elmer Fudd got old after a while. What I did have was a bike, a baseball glove, and a bat. I went *out* to play. I had to. There was nothing to do in my room except sleep and homework. You bet I got out of there. My parents said, "Bill, be home for dinner," and even though I didn't have a cell phone, GPS, or OnStar, I always managed to find my way home in time to set the table.

We had one celebrity resident in Winslow. Strangely enough, this happened to be my father. He was one of the two town doctors, the Dr. Welby of Winslow. In the 1960s and early '70s, doctors were the elite of the elite, the pinnacle of the professional food chain. But I didn't see him as a celebrity. He was just my dad. I did notice that when we walked down the street people would frequently stop him and give him a hug for delivering their twins or saving their lives. I was secretly thrilled and very proud. It was certainly better than having some thug slam your dad up against a wall because he owed him money.

Sometimes if Dad got a call at night, I'd go with him to the hospital or even to someone's home. What's weird is that I had my own scrubs. I don't remember how I got them. Dad probably brought home an extra set and I kept them. I insisted on putting them on every time we went for a house call. I guess I figured that if I wore the scrubs I'd fool people into thinking I was a doctor.

"How old are you now, Bill?"

"Just turned nine."

"And you want to be a doctor like your dad?"

"Nope. I'm a doctor already. I finished medical school last year. I squeezed it in on nights and weekends, between Little League and Cub Scouts."

One thing that wasn't great about having a doctor for a dad was that I could never fake being sick. Most kids have the luxury of grabbing their stomachs in pretend pain and convincing their parents that they need a day at home in bed instead of going to school. As soon as I complained about some bogus stomach pain, Dad would poke around my abdomen, then threaten to give me a shot. I was miraculously cured.

I knew Dad was a great doctor because not only was he smart and good at what he did, he also had a calming bedside manner. He knew just what to say. He was kind, thoughtful, and funny. Both my parents have a great sense of humor, and I like to think I inherited mine from each of them.

One aspect of comedy I know I got from my dad was how to use the element of surprise. One time my mom was sunbathing on a pier near a lake. She was in the process of slathering suntan lotion up and down her arms and legs, and she didn't see Dad drop quietly into the water on the other side of the pier. I covered my mouth because I knew what he was up to. As Mom blissfully rubbed on the lotion, Dad suddenly shot up out of the water and grabbed her foot. Mom screamed. Her fingers reflexively squeezed the tube of suntan lotion. A gob of gooey white lotion spurted right into her hair.

"Damn it, Bill! Now I've got to wash my hair!"

Mom was shouting, but she was also laughing.

I thought Dad's move was brilliant. True, Mom was annoyed and startled, but she wasn't really upset. I could tell because of how hard she was laughing. In fact, Mom and Dad were both laughing hysterically.

I was only in the second grade, but I'd learned my first major comedy lesson: Scaring the crap out of people is funny.

So I began a campaign of trying to frighten everyone I knew, starting with Granddad.

I probably should have considered his age and his health but, well, okay, I didn't. All I thought about was how funny it would be to jump out of the closet and scare him half to death. I was sure that he'd love the joke and fall over laughing. The only problem with Granddad was that he almost never needed anything in the closet. Still, I knew if I snuck in there and exercised extreme patience, eventually he'd open the door.

I pretended to go outside, then doubled back, ducked into the closet, and waited. And waited. I didn't move. Alone in the dark, trapped between two musty winter coats that smelled of mothballs, I stayed in that closet for over an hour. Finally, I heard Grandma say, "Ray, have you seen Willy?"

"He's in the backyard."

"He's been out there a long time."

"You're right. I better see what he's up to."

"Grab your coat. It's getting chilly."

I heard Granddad's boots clopping toward the closet. His footsteps got louder, and then they stopped. I heard the doorknob turning. He opened the door, I leaped out of the dark, and—

"YAAAAAAAAAAAAA!"

Granddad yelped and staggered backward like Mr. Magoo. I thought he was going to fall over the couch, which would have been great, but he steadied himself and glared at me.

"*Willy*! What the—"

"Hey, Granddad. What's for dinner?"

That's the key. You have to be cool, then walk away like nothing happened. 'Course, when I saw Granddad reach for his medication, I got nervous and decided to go after other members of the family next. I did, with much success, hiding in closets, behind doors, and in the bathtub. Finally, I reached the point at which I'd scared everyone in my family, except for the dog. Didn't seem worth it to jump out of the closet and scare old Skeets, although I considered it. I realized that to keep this hilarious joke going, I had to branch out. That meant school.

I actually liked school and got along with most of my teachers. I was the class clown, but I wasn't the kind of clown who was disruptive or disrespectful. I goofed around but within the parameters of the class. That's why most of my teachers liked me. I was a cutup but not a jerk.

I did get sent to the principal twice. The first time was in fourth grade when my buddy dared me to blow my nose on the page of one of my books. Our desks were the type with lift-up lids, perfect for performing weird acts behind the cover of the desktop. But I would never blow my nose in my book without a good reason.

"Hey, Bill."

"Yeah?"

"I dare you to blow your nose in your book."

"You dare me? Well, all right."

I waited for the right moment, lifted the desktop, opened my book, and blew. My buddy broke up, I broke up, the class broke up, and the teacher busted me. He sent me to the principal, who shook his head sadly.

"William, I never would have expected something like this from you. When I tell your father, he's going to be so disappointed."

"Any chance you can leave my father out of this? He has so much on his mind, with healing the sick and saving so many lives. Didn't he come over to your place on a house call recently? I believe so. I was going to come with him but I had to finish my homework before I volunteered at the Veterans Hospital. Oh, wait, that was Tuesday. Tuesdays I help out at Adopt-a-Pet, cleaning the cages—"

"Bill, that'll do."

"Yes, sir."

"And don't use your book for a handkerchief again."

I managed to keep my nose clean for a while, until the following year, when my teacher was Mr. Green, known throughout school as Mean Green. Mr. Green was nasty by nature. He was basically an unhappy man whose attitude seemed to be "I'm miserable teaching you dumb-ass students, so I'm gonna make all of you as miserable as I am."

Every day with Mean Green was an ordeal. Finally, I'd had enough. I decided I had to scare the crap out of him. For his own good. I figured if I jumped out of the closet and scared Mean Green, he'd think this was hilarious and he'd lighten up and become nicer. It didn't occur to me that a ten-year-old jumping out of the closet, screaming like an idiot, might actually make a mean guy meaner. I also didn't think through my plan, or as I called it later: what plan?

I arrived in the classroom before anyone else and slipped into the closet. As soon as my eyes adjusted to the dark, I looked around and saw that the closet was empty. No umbrella, no books, nothing, not even a hanger, which meant there was no reason for Mean Green to open the closet.

I considered my options. I came up with four possibilities, all excellent. One. I could pretend to hang myself up like a coat. Nice touch, but how would that get Mean Green to open the door? Two. I could scratch at the door and start squeaking like a mouse. Clever, but that might just bring in the custodian or, worse, an exterminator who'd spray in rat poison. Three. I could do nothing and rot in here, ending my life in the fifth grade. Four. I could pound on the inside of the closet door. Mean Green would fling open the door, and I'd leap out screaming, still going for the joke. I went for number four.

I pounded on the door and yelled "Help!" a few times; Mean

Green pulled opened the door; I jumped out, howled, did the walka-
way, and nonchalantly sat down at my desk. Mean Green yanked me
up roughly by the arm and tossed me out into the hall. His eyes turned
into alien-like red slits.

"Was that supposed to be some kind of *joke*?"

"Well . . . *yeah*. Didn't you get it?"

"No. Because it wasn't *funny*. I don't think your dad will find it
funny, either."

"Wait, Mean . . . uh, *Mr.* Green—"

"Get out of my face, Funny Boy. Go to the principal's office *now*."
He grunted. "They don't pay me enough for this job."

Okay, I admit it. My comedy career was off to a rocky start.

7. SIX ICE TEAS

My first few years in Winslow, from first grade until third grade, were essentially uneventful. If you take away my penchant for jumping out of closets and scaring people, my life was sickeningly normal. My family was just kind of typical. You'd swear we'd stepped right out of a Norman Rockwell painting or a 1950s TV show. Dad and Mom were just like Ozzie and Harriet, except unlike Ozzie, Dad had a job. My sisters and I got along. We were clean-cut; we went to school, to church, and out to dinner every Sunday night. We were comfortable in every way. Everyone in our family went about his or her business, never rocking the boat.

Sunday nights we made an appearance, along with almost every other family in Winslow, at the Falcon Restaurant, a friendly, family-owned establishment right in the center of town. I ordered the same thing every week: chicken fried steak, mashed potatoes, gravy, and green beans. At first the only complication was our drink order.

"I'll have a Diet Pepsi."

"Coke, please."

"May I have a root beer, no ice? Check that. I'll take a Diet Dr. Pepper."

"I'll have a ginger ale with two ice cubes."

"Root beer, extra ice, and a slice of lemon."

"I'll have the same thing as Janet."

"I'm sorry. Which one is Janet?"

"Janet is the root beer."

"No, I'm not. I *was* the root beer, but I changed. Now I'm the Diet Dr. Pepper. On second thought, I will have a root beer. Actually, make that an orange Shasta—"

"HEY!"

Dad. Immediately, we all shut up. The only sound at our table was our poor waitress scribbling on her order pad like crazy, crossing stuff out, and rewriting our drinks on another sheet of paper. Dad had had enough. "Cancel all the drinks. Just bring us six ice teas, please."

"But I wanted—"

"I don't care what you wanted. You're having ice tea. This poor woman's gonna quit right in the middle of our drink order."

The look on her face told us that Dad was right. She mouthed "thank you" to him, then looked at us and sighed with relief. As she walked away, I thought I heard her mutter, "Life is too short."

By now, you can tell that I looked up to my dad. I never had typical boyhood heroes—ballplayers, rock stars, military generals. Dad was my hero. I wanted to do everything that he did, and just the way he did it, too. The first time we went to the Falcon, Dad got up from the table and walked over to the cash register after dinner to pay the check. I started to get up.

"Where you going?" Mom asked me.

"With Dad."

"You gonna help him pay?"

"Me? No. I'm eight years old. I don't have any money."

"Well, unless you're paying half the bill, sit here and drink your ice tea."

What Mom said made sense. But I made a promise to myself right then, sitting in the old Falcon Restaurant in Winslow, that someday I'd be the one who'd get up from the table and pay the check for Dad. Because I knew if I could do that, he'd be proud of me.

8. BIG FISH

Even though they seemed very different — Dad was a doctor and Granddad drove a Baby Ruth truck—these were the two people who had the most profound effect on me.

First of all, they both provided the same service: making people feel good. It's obvious what a doctor provides, and what's better to lift your spirits than a Baby Ruth candy bar?

My dad was a natural-born healer. He wasn't one of those cold, by-the-numbers doctors with the personality of a piece of wood. Or the other kind I can't stand, the ones with the superior attitude who say, "You're sick, I'm not, I don't like you, I wish I was playing golf." You just knew that Dad would make you better and you knew that he cared. I hope that's one quality that I've inherited from him: his ability to care about people.

The thing about Granddad that's always stuck with me is that he loved life. Whatever he was doing at the time was absolutely the best thing there was to do. While he was driving his Baby Ruth truck, he was the happiest, best Baby Ruth truck driver in the world. *Love what you're doing*. That's what I learned from Granddad.

I once watched Granddad shave. Man, did he take his time. He studied himself in the mirror, then made a whole ritual of slapping on preshave lotion. Then he lathered up his shaving cream and spread it all over his face like clouds of whipped cream. Once he began actually shaving, he slid his razor up and down his face in a series of slow, deliberate motions. Satisfied that his face was as smooth as a baby's bottom, he splashed on aftershave, finally ending the whole deal by giving himself a mini facial massage.

"Don't you hate shaving?" I asked him. "You have to go through all this every day."

"Well, here's what I do, Willy," Granddad said. "I pretend that every time I shave it's the first time." He wiped his face down now with a hot towel, then sighed with pure pleasure. "I figure if I have to shave, I might as well enjoy it."

That was his attitude and one of the valuable lessons I learned from him. I hope.

I have wonderful memories of visiting my grandparents in Texas. Grandma was famous for two things: her chocolate cake and playing the organ. When Dad said, "Pack up your things, Bill, we're going to Granddad's for the weekend," I would imagine myself in Grandma's kitchen. I would picture Grandma's chocolate cake sitting on the counter with icing so thick it was almost the size of a second cake itself, and my mouth would literally start to water.

Then I would see her sitting at the organ in her living room and I'd hear her screeching *"Amaaazzzzzing Graaaaaace"* at the top of her lungs, and I'd shudder. Even though her singing and playing were always inhumanely loud and painful to the point that most of the neighborhood dogs came running to the back door and howled along with her, she sang with such joy that I learned to love music simply because she loved music so much. The music she heard herself play was obviously in a different register than the music we heard her play, but it didn't matter. What mattered was how she threw herself into each song with total abandon. The music moved her. And while it moved me in a different way—it moved me to cover my ears—it also made me see how music can come from a place that's deep within you. That's where the term "soul music" comes from. I love music; I play some painful guitar myself, and I listen to music constantly. I thank my grandmother for giving me that gift.

Another life lesson I took away from both Dad and Granddad is that life is more rewarding if you think of the other person first and yourself second. I learned this the first time I ever went fishing.

Dad and Granddad had pulled me out of bed at the ungodly hour of 5:00 A.M. and dragged me to the local fishing hole. They'd decided to make a day of it. Grandma had made us lunch, and Dad and Granddad had packed us drinks in a cooler, along with a big piece of chocolate cake. I wore a fishing hat and boots, and Granddad had given me my own fishing rod. Everything was perfect.

Except the fish weren't biting. I changed lures, tried fresh bait, attached a new hook. Nothing. Not a single fish. Not even a minnow.

We fished for hours. The longer we fished, the more my spirits sank. I wanted to catch something, anything, my first time out, but it was getting late and I was getting tired and bored.

"Fishing's not that much fun if you don't catch anything," I said.

"You'll catch something," Granddad promised. "You just have to wait 'em out. See, the fish know what you're doing. It's like a war of wills."

"They can win. I don't care."

"What kind of attitude is that for a fisherman?" Dad said.

"Maybe I'm not a fisherman," I said.

Dad and Granddad exchanged a look but said nothing.

"I have to pee," I said. I handed Dad my fishing rod, got up, and headed toward some bushes. When I came back a minute later, I was pretty much done with fishing.

"Can we go home?"

"Give it five more minutes," Dad said.

I sighed and took my fishing pole from him.

Suddenly I felt something tugging at my line. It happened so fast that I wasn't sure it had happened at all.

"He's got something!" Dad shouted.

"Hold on, Willy!" Granddad hollered.

"I think you landed a big one," Dad said.

I felt my line go limp; then, using all my strength, I yanked my fishing pole out of the water. Dangling from the hook was a large perch.

"What a beauty!" Dad said.

"Your first one, too," Granddad said. "Amazing."

I was panicked. "What do I do?"

"Just lay it on the ground and we'll pull it off the hook," Dad said.

"No way," I said.

"What?" Dad said.

"I have to show it to Grandma. Then I'm gonna take it home and show Mom, the girls, and all my friends."

"But Bill, you have to take it off the hook—"

"I can't. They won't believe I caught it."

Dad and Granddad looked at each other.

"It's gonna really stink," Dad said.

"I don't care. It's my first fish."

Dad and Granddad looked at each other again.

"Well, okay," Dad said.

I grinned and started running toward my grandparents' house, the perch still hanging from my pole.

What I didn't know was that when I had gone off to pee, Dad had seen the dead perch floating on top of the water. He grabbed it and hooked it to my line.

I dragged the dead fish around with me all day. Finally, even I couldn't take the stink. I settled for a Polaroid Granddad took of me holding up my fish as I grinned toothlessly at the camera, the proudest kid on the planet.

Dad eventually told me the truth. Deep inside I knew that I never caught that fish.

Heck, I was twenty-seven when he told me.

9. TEARS OF
A CLOWN

I've always been a music guy. In fact, growing up in Winslow, about the only activity I enjoyed doing inside, other than eating half of Grandma's chocolate cake in one sitting, was listening to the radio or playing record albums. I was heavy into rock 'n' roll.

The first single I bought on my own was "Tears of a Clown" by Smokey Robinson. The first album I ever bought with my own money was *Three Dog Night Live at the Forum*. I was obsessed with them. Just *loved* them. Practically wore out that record. One of my sick friends, Danny Case, told me that his dad wrote "Jeremiah Was a Bullfrog." I not only believed Danny, I told everybody that my friend's dad was a famous songwriter. Yes. I was an idiot.

At night, I used to get in bed and turn on the greatest rock radio station ever, KOMA in Oklahoma City. They'd play rock music all night long and I would listen and sing along until eventually I fell asleep. At that age, I was more than a little naive and gullible. I actually thought the bands came into the station, played their song, packed up their stuff, and left, making way for the next band. I thought every song was played live, in-studio! I'd lie in bed, drifting off to sleep, and I'd think, *How do they get all those bands in there? It's amazing!*

A few months later, I won a radio contest sponsored by little KINO in Winslow, a tiny AM station. On the air, the DJ asked easy questions like which band sang which song. I knew the answer to a particular question, called up the station, and won. The prize was a trip to the station and fifty records. I was so excited. Of course, now I know that the station was just clearing out its inventory, but at the time, I felt like I hit Lotto.

One afternoon I drove my bike over to KINO, which was a small cinder block of a building at the far edge of Winslow. The first thing I wondered when I went inside and saw that the entire radio station consisted of a tiny glassed-in control room and a minuscule waiting room with one battered sofa was *How do the bands fit in here?*

I asked the DJ. He stared at me as if I were a sad, simple child who'd obviously been dropped on his head when he was an infant.

"Uh, son," he said, speaking slowly so I could understand him. "The bands don't come in here. We play *records*."

He held one up so I could see what he was talking about. "It's this round vinyl thing with a hole in the middle."

"Got it," I said, nodding like the moron he thought I was.

I ran out of there before he told me something I didn't want to know about the Tooth Fairy and the Easter Bunny.

10. HOT DOG BUBBLE GUM

Recently, I was out to dinner with my wife and two other couples. We'd each had two or three or seven adult beverages, and the conversation was free-flowing and loose. We started talking about our dreams and our regrets, the goals we'd accomplished and the opportunities we'd missed. Someone asked, "If you could wave a magic wand and start all over, what would you change about your life?"

"I'd change one little thing," I said. "I'd have become a Major League baseball player."

The guys nodded, completely understanding,

thinking I was awesome. The women shook their heads, thinking I was ridiculous.

"I used to be really good," I said. "I was Home Run King."

"Forty years ago," my wife clarified. "In Little League."

More head shaking from the women.

"Hey, when I was a kid, Little League was everything. Little League was *life.*"

And it was.

B
efore I fell head over heels in love with baseball, I had brief flings with other sports and outdoor activities. I began with basketball. Dad hung a hoop in our driveway in Winslow. A hoop in your driveway is like a magnet. My friends started coming over every day after school and on weekends, and we'd play pickup games.

Basketball is a great game, especially if you've got some height. If you don't have height, you ought to have some quickness and a good eye.

I was short, slow, and I couldn't throw a rock into the ocean.

But I was enthusiastic, aggressive, and able to commit an infinite number of fouls in a very short time, which resulted in guys saying things like "Hey, Engvall, this is a basketball game, not a mugging," or "You guarding me or dancing with me?" or "Nice shot, Engvall. Never saw anyone shoot a lay-up that actually went *over* the garage."

I quit basketball and decided to join the Cub Scouts. I'm not sure why, except that every other kid in Winslow was a Cub Scout, so I figured it was the cool thing to do. Wasn't that cool. I did learn how to tie a slip knot and how to make a fire by rubbing two sticks together, two skills that so far have rarely come in handy.

We did have fun on the campouts. Except right before we turned in for the night, our scoutmaster came into our tent and told me and my buddy to put our underwear outside on the tent pole. He said that since you'd been sweating in your drawers all day, the night air would act as a refrigerant and cool and clean them naturally. This actually made a lot of sense. One problem. There was just no way my buddy and I were going to hang our dirty underwear outside on our tent pole.

"I ain't taking off my underwear," my buddy said.

"You never do," I said.

Bottom line, we put our clean underwear out on the tent pole and left our dirty underwear on.

I'm sure the scoutmaster was right about the cold night air acting as a cleansing agent. It was just weird.

And I'm not into weird.

At first we played sandlot ball, just a bunch of guys, nothing organized. We played every summer day, doubleheaders, even tripleheaders, until it got too dark to see. We baked in the hot sun, shirtless, our shirts and spare gloves the bases, the dust kicking up into small, blinding storms as we rounded first, trying to stretch a single into a double. We had no umps, didn't call balls or strikes. We played the game on the honor system. We argued if we thought we were safe, but we never fought. We all knew that it was just a game.

We dreamed of Little League, which to us kids in Winslow equaled the Show. We had no T-ball, five-pitch, or pre–Little League. Once you turned eight, you tried out for Little League, and basically if you could walk, you were put on a team.

The first team I played on was the Cardinals. I had a full uniform—pants, socks, and shirt with my name stitched on the back—but the best part was the shoes, metal cleats. There is nothing better than the sound of metal cleats on concrete. I would put on my uniform and stroll up and down the concrete walkway outside the ball field before games just to hear my cleats clatter. Made me feel like a Major Leaguer.

Like most ballplayers, I was superstitious. I approached every game the same way. Had to. If I didn't, I knew I'd go into a season-long slump or commit a million errors in the field. My ritual wasn't elaborate: I laid out my uniform the night before, front side up. It looked like a little flat man. Then I oiled my mitt, always tying a base-ball into the pocket overnight to keep my glove loose and flexible. I couldn't wait for the game. I can still remember the smell of the freshly mowed grass on the field and the woodchips on the walkway.

The ball field had wooden bleachers. My dad came to as many games as he could, but being a doctor, he was often tied up saving someone's life. Flimsy excuse. Mom managed to come to every game. She had to. She was the scorekeeper.

Dad happened to make the first game I ever played. It was a night game, but the air was still hot and sticky despite the dark sky. My second at-bat, I reached first base when the opposing third baseman, shortstop, second baseman, and pitcher all circled under my weak pop-up and somehow the ball came down in the middle of all of them, untouched. Maybe they all lost it in the lights. Didn't matter to me. In the box score I kept in my head, I'd just ripped a liner to left.

I started dancing off first, trying to distract the pitcher. He paid absolutely no attention to me. It was as if I didn't exist. This bothered me. I decided right then that I was going to steal second. If he's gonna give it to me, might as well take it. And if he doesn't pay me any attention, I'll steal third. Maybe rob home, too.

I took a big lead. The pitcher went into his windup and I burst into motion, streaking toward second. I had a monster jump. Oh, I had this baby *nabbed.* Put one into the stolen base column in my mental stat sheet.

I went into my slide, my spikes kicking up a mini dust tornado, and . . .

I landed five feet short of the bag.

The catcher came up throwing. He gunned the ball to the shortstop, who tagged me out while I was still lying in a heap, a mile short of second base.

I could hear the crowd roar. Then I could hear them laugh.

Then I could feel the tears leaking down my face.

Suddenly my mind went into overdrive and I grabbed my leg.

"Oww," I howled. "I think I broke my ankle."

A hush came over the crowd, and within five seconds I saw a figure looming over me.

Dad.

He looked at the group of baseball players, my teammates, who were starting to gather around me. He gestured for them to move back. "It's okay," he said. "I'm a doctor." Then he squatted next to me.

"Ow," I said meekly.

Dad spoke in a whisper. "Son, I know your ankle's not hurt."

"Umm," I said.

"I know you're just embarrassed."

I started to argue, but, of course, he was right.

"Now," Dad said, "I want you to get up and walk to the dugout like a man, all right?"

I nodded. He helped me to my feet. I pretended to limp a little, and then, with the crowd applauding, I broke into a slow, painful jog. For my final, crowning touch, I tipped my cap to the crowd. Then I disappeared into the dugout.

My coach, Walt Maul, was waiting for me at the bench. "You okay?"

"Yeah. I think I walked it off."

"Good."

"It feels almost completely healed. I can keep playing."

"Great. Oh, by the way, that slide?"

"Yeah?"

"Funniest thing I ever seen."

———

Nothing beats baseball. Even a bad baseball game is better than no baseball game. There's a slogan the marketing people came up with for Major League Baseball: "I live for this." That describes me to a T, especially when I was back in Winslow.

Baseball was more than my favorite game and my favorite way to spend time. It was my social life. I hung out with the guys on my team even when we didn't have a game. My buddies and I would sit on the bench for hours, talking, laughing, and goofing around. Our dugout was our clubhouse, our hangout, our Cheers bar.

At the end of every game, win or lose, our team went out for a treat. It was never anything elaborate. Usually we just went to the snack bar next to the bleachers and each got to choose one thing. I always chose the same treat: hot dog bubble gum. Actually this was just regular old bubble gum in the shape of a little hot dog, but I thought it was the greatest snack ever invented. In fact, I would buy two or three pieces of hot dog bubble gum *before* the game and chomp on them while we played. Having a big ol' wad of hot dog bubble gum packed into your cheek while you were sitting on the bench solving the problems of third grade? The best.

We'd pretend we were Major Leaguers, scratch ourselves, spit, and relive the highlights—and lowlights—of games past. One of the best involved a kid named Ross Dover. Ross was older than I was. He played on the Dodgers. Ross was tall and gangly and had a shock of long, straggly hair. He was our local hippie. He reminded me of Reverend Jim on the TV show *Taxi*. I don't think Ross ever did drugs; he just looked and sounded as if he did. He didn't march to a different drummer; he marched to a completely different band.

We were playing the Dodgers one afternoon, and Ross was in center field. We were at bat. I was on deck. The guy at the plate swung at the first pitch and sent a lazy fly ball to center. Ross barely had to move to haul it in. He put his glove up and—*boink*—the ball plunked him right on top of the head. Ross sort of stared for a second, standing still as a statue; then a goofy grin came over his face. He looked down at the ball, which had trickled a few feet away, picked it up, threw it in, and passed out.

"Whoa," I said from the on-deck circle.

People started running out toward Ross. Suddenly, he sat up, waved everybody away, got to his feet, and pounded his fist into his glove, ready to field his position as if nothing had happened. Knowing Ross, it's possible that he never knew that the ball hit him and he was out cold. I think he was used to being in that state of mind.

11. THE BEST DAY OF MY LIFE

Of course, the best day of my life centered on baseball. I can even identify the best *moment* of my life. It was the moment I came of age in baseball:

My first home run.

Eventually I became known as a home run hitter. As I played baseball for a few years, into Babe Ruth League, I actually made All-Stars. I was a left-handed power hitter, and after a slow start I began cranking balls out of that Winslow Little League field with some regularity. I had a home run swing, a quick uppercut, and even though I wasn't the biggest player on the field, no Boog

Powell, I was wiry. It's all in the wrists anyway. At least that's what they say. I just know I hit my fair share of homers.

But none was as sweet as that first one.

To begin with, before I hit a home run, I didn't think I could. I had no reason to believe I had home run power. I never hit one. I got good wood on the ball a few times, but all I hit was long foul balls or long outs.

My Dad was at this game, too, when it happened for the first time. Good thing. He was able to describe my home run to me, since I never really saw it.

I swung hard, and I felt the ball fly off my bat. I saw the center fielder go back. He was looking up, but the ball was only as high as his eyes. Still, he kept going back.

Maybe, I thought as I ran toward first. *Just maybe.*

The ball sailed an inch above the center fielder's glove, grazed the top of the fence, and dribbled over.

It was official. I had hit the puniest home run ever.

Dad's first reaction was, "How did the center fielder not catch that?"

His second reaction was, "Wait, wait, wait! Bill just hit a *home run!*"

I didn't believe it. I didn't believe it so much that I never went into a home run trot. I sprinted around the bases. I wanted to touch home before they called it back, said it wasn't a homer because it touched the fence, or found some other excuse not to let me have it.

But nothing like that happened. I tagged home plate, and my teammates rushed me. That was a feeling I wanted to experience again. And there was something else I knew:

There's no such thing as a cheap home run.

After that first one, I made sure that when I hit one out, there was never any doubt. It was *gone.*

Like the next time I came up in that same game. First pitch. I whaled on it. Met the pitcher's fastball with the meat of my bat. The ball shot off like a rocket. This time I knew. So did everyone else. This time the center fielder just turned his back, placed his glove on his hip, and watched the ball sail a mile over his head, over the fence, and into the parking lot

As I trotted around the bases, I smiled at Dad, who was on his feet, applauding along with the other Cardinal parents, and as I rounded third, I smiled at Mom, who was clapping her hands at the score-keeper's table. Our eyes met, and she raised both her arms in triumph.

The whole team was waiting for me at home plate. They mobbed me as if I had hit the homer that won the World Series.

It was incredible, almost surreal. Two home runs in one game! I was beyond happy. I was giddy.

And I had no idea that my world was about to come crashing down.

12. THE WORST DAY OF MY LIFE

Ironically, the worst day of my life and the best day of my life were the same day.

The day I hit my two home runs, I raced into our house, higher than a kite. We didn't have a video camera or instant replay, so the only way I could sear this game into my memory forever was to talk about it.

And talk about it I did. Talked to my parents and my sisters, and then, when they couldn't take it anymore, I talked to the dog. I finally took a shower and changed out of my uniform. When I came out of my room and headed into the kitchen for a snack, my father intercepted me. He had a look on his face as if someone had died.

"I want you to come into the living room," he said. "Your mother and I need to talk to you."

I bounced into the living room, still high, oblivious to what was about to happen. I saw that my father was standing stiffly in the middle of the room. He cleared his throat and shifted his weight as if he were trying to find his balance. Mom sat in an overstuffed armchair. She was leaning forward, her hands clasped in her lap. The color had drained from her face. She was ashen, her mouth set in a thin creased line. She looked like she was frozen or made of wax.

My sisters were all clumped together on the couch. They were tickling each other, clueless, unaccustomed to being called together for any sort of family meeting, especially one like this, one that had something big, something *momentous*, stamped all over it. I couldn't fathom what was about to happen.

Dad cleared his throat again, louder, a signal for us to settle down. My sisters squirmed on the couch, then pushed themselves back into the cushions.

There was a long pause. The silence was eerie, the calm before the hurricane. I looked at my father. He was starting to speak, then he stopped. It seemed as if he were grappling to find the precise words. I found myself losing focus. In my mind, I drifted back to the ball field, engulfed again in the sweet, innocent image of my two home runs, the biggest accomplishment of my life. I was circling the bases, seeing Dad in the stands, Mom at the scorer's table—

"Your mother's leaving us."

Dad's voice. But not a voice I'd ever heard before. Dad had a clear, DJ's voice. This voice was thin, lifeless. Just words.

"She's moving out," he said flatly, then quickly added: "Not this minute. Not today. In a few days."

I blinked, once, twice, peered at my sisters. Janet, the oldest at seven, looked at me, and she, too, blinked, then searched Dad's face. Judy and Jenny seemed unaware, uncomprehending. None of us, even our parents, especially our parents, knew what to do now.

I looked at Mom. She had not moved. She sat frozen, still as a statue. I wanted her to say *something*. I wanted her to leap out of that chair and tell us that this was a joke or a bad dream. Instead she dropped her head and stared at her hands in her lap. Her face crinkled slightly as if she were noticing her hands for the first time.

"So, yeah, that's the story. That's how it's gonna be."

Dad shifted his weight again and then suddenly clapped his hands. I jumped at the noise. Dad wasn't sure what else to say or what else to do. He wanted to change the subject, change the mood.

"All right. I think we have a couple of home runs to celebrate. Who wants to get some ice cream?"

It hit me then. And not until then. The reality of it, the absoluteness of it.

My parents were splitting up. My mother was not going to live with us anymore.

I suddenly felt afraid—and alone. Then I felt something moist on my cheeks and I heard a kind of low howl, which I realized came from my throat. Then I started to sob, loud, deep sobs, and I wanted to hug my mother and my father but I couldn't, I just couldn't. I wanted to stop this. I wanted this not to be happening.

Then my mom moaned, and I saw that she, too, was crying. She cried soundlessly, and still she had not moved.

"Well, all right, I know it's—" My father's voice drifted off, ensnared by yet another catch in his throat. He battled through it and managed, "Come on, let's go. Good to get out. Have some ice cream."

It was crazy. All of it. When did this happen? How could it happen? Dad, always so thoughtful and careful and intelligent, the fixer of strangers' hearts, had just broken mine. Mom, helpless, sat pinned in her overstuffed armchair, suddenly looking small and frail, buried her face in her hands and sobbed.

The rest is a blur. I cried, the tears soaking my shirt, and Mom and I hugged, clinging to each other, and then I was in the car, riding next to my dad, the silence in the car as thick as the silence in a tomb. At the ice cream shop, we ordered quickly, the flavors we always did, cones for all of us kids. Dad hustled us outside, trying to avoid encountering anyone he knew. In the parking lot, leaning against our car, my sisters, their giddiness returned, eagerly lapped up their ice cream cones while I stared at mine, mesmerized, lost in space, watching my ice cream drip over the side of my cone, melting away, just as I had ten minutes before witnessed a part of my life melt away and disappear forever.

13. CLEMENTINE

I stumbled through the next three weeks in a kind of cloud. I felt as if my whole identity had changed. I'd gone from Bill, a regular, normal kid, the kid who made you laugh and who could slam home runs, to Bill, that kid whose parents are breaking up, the one standing over there in a daze.

Back then, in Winslow in the 1960s, you didn't talk about things like divorce. We didn't have shrinks or therapy; people didn't let out their feelings. You kept your feelings inside, where they belonged. Especially if you were a guy, even an eight-year-old guy. So I did what I had to do. I sucked it up, kept everything bottled up. I'm not sure who I would've talked to even if I'd wanted to talk.

The closest person we had to a shrink was Pojo Powell, our Little League umpire and our local barber. I suppose Pojo would've been the logical choice because he worked on your head. Plus he liked to talk and offer advice and opinions. I can imagine what confiding in him about my parents' divorce would've been like.

"Hey, Billy Boy, you're up next."

"Hi, Pojo."

"Same as always? Buzz cut?"

"Sure, whatever. I don't really care."

"You sound kinda down. Something bothering you? You know you can always talk to me."

"Really?"

"You bet."

"Well, okay. My parents are getting a divorce. I'm pretty broke up about it."

"That's rough. Not too many divorces around here. Can't say why that is. Don't know what I'd do if my wife left me. I know it'd mess me up, I'll tell you that."

"Maybe we should talk about something else—"

"Yeah, divorce is rough. Always fallout. Hey, I got an idea. Take your mind off things. The new *Boys' Life* just came in. Article in there about baseball. 'Keeping Your Foot Out of the Bucket.' Some good tips."

"Thanks. I'll read it later."

"Suit yourself."

"Well, thanks for talking to me about divorce, Pojo."

"Yeah, good talk. Any time. I'm here for you, bud."

———

Two things kept me sane during that time.

The first was baseball.

None of the guys on my team said anything to me, and I didn't feel comfortable saying anything to them, but I knew that they knew. It was the *not* talking about it with them that worked for me. Somehow I knew that if I did feel like talking about the divorce, I could, at least to my closest friends on the team. I just never felt like it. But there were things, small things, that showed me that the guys were thinking about me and they cared: an extra pat on the back, someone grabbing my glove for me, and a couple of times guys just handed me wads of hot dog bubble gum for no reason. I knew they were there.

Having the routine of baseball, knowing that I had a game to play, gave me something to look forward to and count on. I needed that since I wasn't sure what else I could count on. When your mom and dad announce that they're splitting up, life itself feels as if it's been tipped over on you.

The second thing that kept me sane, or at least kept me focused, was the third-grade play, "Clementine," in which I played the title character. I know. Clementine is a girl. I didn't care. All I knew was that I tried out and I got the *lead*. Girl, boy, Martian, it didn't matter. I was playing the title role! Of course I thought that my teacher, Mrs. Fields, had cast me as Clementine because I was such a fine actor. I found out later that my voice was too high to play a cowboy, so I either played Clementine or handed out programs. Since this was such a sensitive time for me, Mrs. Fields wisely decided not to saddle me with any further rejection.

The whole process of my parents' separating was confusing. After telling us that they were splitting up, my parents spent the next two weeks not splitting up. They slept in separate rooms, spoke rarely, ate at different times, but they still lived in the same house. I wasn't sure what to think or how to act. I wanted to say to my dad, "I thought you said Mom was leaving. How come she's still here? Does this mean it was a mistake?"

About a week before the play, Mom finally moved out. She found a place on the other side of town. She told us it was temporary. In a few weeks, she was going to move to Flagstaff, an hour away.

It was official and it was real. My mother was gone. The house felt empty and cold and sad. Deeply sad. Dad felt that way, too. I knew because at night when I was practicing my lines for "Clementine" and going through my song, I'd hear Dad go into his room, close the door, and cry.

At first I wasn't sure what I was hearing. I had never heard Dad cry. The idea of Dad crying was so foreign, so out of character. He was the one who comforted other people when they were upset. I'd seen him do that a dozen times. Hearing him cry scared me. I felt like I should do something. The first time I heard him cry, I actually tiptoed out of my room and listened outside his door. I was tempted to go into his room, but I didn't know what I would say. I thought I heard him stop. I tiptoed back into my room, but then I heard a low soft whimper. I got into bed and I could still hear him. Lying there, staring at the ceiling, trying to make sense of all of this, I realized that Dad was hurting as much as I was and he needed to cry.

I knew I needed to cry, too. I just couldn't. It was as if I had two conflicting emotions crashing into each other. On the one hand, I felt as if I should cry. Dad cried, and I didn't know anyone who was more of a guy's guy than Dad. On the other hand, if I cried, especially in front of anybody, wouldn't I be seen as a baby, less of a man somehow?

Now I'm going to admit something here. Something only those really close to me know.

I'm a crier.

I cry when my kids do almost anything. Doesn't have to be because one of them hits the winning basket or has a dance solo in the spotlight. I cry when they're warming up.

I cry when I hear a sad song. Can be a current song or a song I remember from when I was a kid. Can be a song that you wouldn't think would set me off, like "Mandy" by Barry Manilow. As soon as I hear the opening notes, forget it. I'm a puddle.

Worst of all, I cry at movies. I try not to. I try to hold back. But it's hopeless. It doesn't even have to be a movie in which someone dies. In fact, the movie that caused the biggest waterworks for me, maybe ever, was *Finding Nemo*. When the Albert Brooks fish found Nemo? I was a goner. I started wailing. Thankfully Gail and I were in the dark, so I could deny it.

"Bill?"

"Huh?"

"Are you crying?"

"Me? Naw. Something flew in my eye. You got a tissue?"

"You are crying."

"I don't cry. I'm from Texas. Shoot, I think a bug flew in there. Can . . . you . . . please . . . hand me . . . a . . . waaaaaaaaAAAAAA."

Right about then everyone in the theater handed me a tissue.

I managed to keep it together the entire week before our performance of "Clementine." Starring as Clementine was in itself sort of surreal, starting with the costume fitting. All the other boys were dressed as cowboys. I was wearing a long yellow dress and a blond wig with two long braids. I think I knew instinctively that just coming out in that costume would bring the house down. Even at eight years old I was not above going for a sure, cheap laugh.

After I got dressed, about five minutes before the play, I glanced at the parents taking their seats in the classroom, and I saw my parents sitting together in the front row. I blinked twice. They were next to each other, but they might as well have been sitting a mile apart. It was so obvious that they were never going to get together. Why did they have to be together now?

I just lost it. I started crying uncontrollably, unleashing three weeks of pent-up tears. The principal, who was standing in the back of the classroom, made his way toward me and took me aside, out of earshot.

"You have to hold it together, son."

"I'm . . . try . . . trying"

"Bill," he said, "the show must go on."

I looked at him uncomprehendingly. This was a *third-grade* play, not opening night of *Cats* on Broadway.

I don't remember what else he said or how I managed to pull myself together, but somehow I grabbed hold of my long yellow dress, climbed up on Mrs. Fields's desk, which was supposed to be a table in a saloon, and belted out a heartbreaking, show-stopping "Oh, my darlin', oh my darlin', oh my darlin' Clementine," as if I were an eight-year-old Bette Midler.

The show ended to huge applause and a standing ovation, with Mom and Dad the first ones on their feet, clapping and cheering the loudest.

I don't know why, but I knew then that even though Mom and Dad would be going their separate ways, everything would be all right. Somehow.

I also knew that I was destined to become either a comedian or a cross-dresser.

14. TURKEY SHOOT

S hortly after my star turn in "Clementine," Mom moved to Flagstaff, and my
grandparents moved in with us. While
Mom's leaving left a giant hole in my
heart and in our family, we didn't dwell on the
loss. We couldn't. There was too much going on,
too much chaos. Our household was now bursting
with three adults and four superactive kids, and
Dad was busier than ever. For some reason, that
year everyone in Winslow came down with sore
throats at three in the morning. He must've felt
the need to escape and get some quality male

bonding, because he arranged a hunting trip for just the two of us. A six-day father-and-son turkey shoot.

It began with no turkey and no shooting. For five days we didn't see a feather. We sat in the woods, perched with our rifles, waiting. Mostly we shot the breeze since there was nothing else to shoot. It didn't matter to me. I was just happy to have this time with Dad.

On our last day out, Dad decided to break camp early and head back to Winslow. We shoved all our stuff into the back of his pickup and started driving out of the woods through a maze of dusty logging roads. We left plenty of time because, being guys, we knew it was guaranteed that we'd get lost. This was before MapQuest and GPS systems, not that we would have used either of them even if they existed—

We drove down a dirt road, which intersected another identical dirt road, then drove up that one, thinking that we were about to connect to the main highway.

"Yep, this is it," Dad said, as the pickup skidded through dust. We headed down this road . . . and arrived at the same dirt road where we started.

"Damn," Dad said, lifting up his ball cap and scratching his head. "Oh, I know. It's this way," and drove confidently up yet another dirt road.

After about an hour of going in circles, Dad veered off the road we were on, nodded, and headed back down another road, one that looked exactly like the one we just left.

"This is the way," he said. "I recognize that tree."

"Oh yeah," I said, squinting at a tree that looked like every other tree we'd passed.

Suddenly, a turkey the size of a small cow darted into the road, right in front of us. Dad slammed on the brakes. The truck screeched to a stop. I braced myself against the dashboard with both hands. Dad reached behind him for his rifle, jumped out of the truck, aimed the rifle, and shot the turkey. I climbed out of the cab, my mouth opened wide in shock, thinking, *My father has lost his mind.*

He held his hand up, a stop sign. "Stand back, son," he said in a low voice. "The turkey's not dead yet."

"What do we do?"

"I can't let it suffer."

I took a step farther back as Dad pulled out his pistol and shot the turkey right in the head. I winced. Dad whistled.

"Well, at least we got ourselves a turkey," he said.

Soon after, we found the main highway and drove back to Winslow. Once we got home, Dad carried the turkey into our house, and we started plucking it over the kitchen sink. As we yanked out the feathers, something strange caught my eye:

There was only one bullet hole in the bird. A small hole. From a pistol.

"I'm confused," I said.

"About what?"

"There's only one bullet hole."

For the briefest moment, Dad drummed his fingers on the side of the sink. He stared at the small hill of feathers that had accumulated on the newspaper on the kitchen counter, his eyes narrow in concentration. He didn't speak for a few seconds.

What I realized much later was that he was concocting a story. Some guys tell fish tales. Dad was inventing a whole new genre, the turkey tale. His tale was based on a scientific fact that I had not yet learned:

You can literally scare a turkey to death.

Jamming on the truck's brakes and screeching to a stop in front of the turkey had given the poor gobbler a heart attack. The bird had passed away from cardiac arrest.

"I know," Dad said finally. "I know there's only one hole."

"But you shot the turkey *twice*."

"Yep."

Dad smiled at me patiently, a man who at all times exuded intelligence and inspired faith.

"I didn't want to ruin the meat, so I put the second bullet through the original hole," he said.

"Oh," I said, nodding, believing that Dad was not only the smartest dad in the world, but also the best shot.

Aren't all dads?

15. HORMONES ON THE RANGE

Around fifth grade, I discovered girls.

I had always known about them, but had never paid much attention to them except to annoy and torture them, the way I did my sisters. Suddenly something happened. I can't put my finger on what it was, or when it did. It just did. One day I had a whole new perspective. I looked at girls and something *stirred*. I liked them in a different way, and I wanted them to like me in a different way. That's about all I knew, but it was enough.

One morning before school, Dad asked me to stay at home that night with my sisters. He was going out and he didn't want them to be alone. I shrugged, told him sure. I had nothing else to do.

That afternoon, a girl in my class, Natalie, asked me if I wanted to go to the movies that night. Now Natalie was hot. She had long black hair and an olive complexion, and the rumor was that she was fast. I wasn't sure what that meant, but I knew it had nothing to do with running. With my new attitude toward girls, the moment Natalie asked me to go with her to the movies, I forgot all about babysitting my sisters and blurted out, "What time?"

The plan was to meet Natalie at seven in the balcony. Dad had gone out an hour before. I told my sisters I had forgotten something at school and I'd be back in an hour. I set them up in front of the TV and headed to the movie theater.

Natalie was waiting for me. The moment the lights went down, she was all over me. I had never kissed a girl before. It was pretty clear that Natalie had kissed plenty of boys, because the first thing she did was jam her tongue into my mouth. I had no idea what she was doing. At first I was freaked out. My dad was a doctor, and I'd never heard of anything like this. It was borderline disgusting, then it was pretty nice, and then it was just excellent. Even if what we were doing was unsanitary and weird and kinky, there was no way I was stopping.

Then a thought hit me and I got really scared.

What if Natalie got pregnant?

That's how little I knew about sex.

There was only one thing to do. Ask the sex expert: Richard Nunez.

Richard was the catcher on our baseball team. Richard was my age but looked about thirty. I think he shaved between innings. By the third grade, Richard had become an expert on sex because he had older brothers. If you had a question, you asked Richard. He'd set you straight.

The next day I went to the baseball field after school and found Richard in his usual spot, sitting in the dugout. The dugout was kind of like Richard's office. I sat down next to him. You had to be cool when you talked to Nunez. He had all the answers when it came to women, but he might not give you any information if he thought you were a geek. We kidded around a little, then I broached the subject. I told him about French kissing Natalie and how I was worried that she was pregnant. Richard burst out laughing.

"Engvall, you're pathetic," he said. "You have to have sex with a girl three times before she can get pregnant."

Richard now has twelve kids and can't figure out why.

But back then, after talking to Nunez, I felt an enormous sense of relief. At least I knew I was not about to become a ten-year-old father.

My feeling of relief lasted from the moment I left the baseball field until I walked through our front door, a grand total of seven minutes. Dad was waiting for me. The half-smile on his face said that I was in pile of trouble.

"Hey, Bill," he said.

"Hi, Dad."

"Anything you want to tell me?"

"Let's see . . . nope. I think you're pretty much up to date on everything. Well, gotta do my homework, then I've got to get going on my chores. Maybe I'll wash the car, too, and I'm thinking about painting the garage."

I started toward my room.

"How was the movie?"

Dad's voice was flat, matter-of-fact. This was always a bad thing. It signaled major punishment up ahead.

"Movie? Which movie? You mean the one the girls and I watched last night on TV?"

"No. The one you went out to last night when you were supposed to be *here,* taking care of your sisters."

"Oh, *that* movie. Disappointing. Gene Shalit was totally wrong about it. I didn't stay. I was only there for maybe five minutes—"

"Bill, you were spotted by almost everyone in town. You came in when the lights went down, and you left when the lights came up. And what were you doing in the balcony, anyway?"

Sometimes there's a downside to living in a small town.

16. I FOUGHT THE LAW

For the most part, I was a good kid. Never got in much trouble. This was not because I was Mr. Clean; this was based solely on survival instinct. It was a matter of risk versus reward. I discovered early on that the punishment I received was always way worse than the pleasure I got committing the crime. With the exception of sneaking out to the movies and getting French-kissed by Natalie.

The real problem was that I was just bad at being bad. Some people have a knack of getting away with stuff. I don't. If there was a 99.9 percent chance of getting away with something, I'd fall right into that .1 percent. Every time. If I was the driver of the get-away car, I'd turn on the ignition, the car would stall out, the engine would flood, the cops would surround us, and I'd go to prison for life with a cellmate named Bubba.

I'm not sure whether I was unlucky or the plans I hatched were dumb. Some of both, I guess. I just know that if you were a gambler, you could've made a fortune betting that I'd get caught. It was uncanny.

I had just gotten a new minibike, something I'd been dying for. I wanted to drive it immediately. We lived right near the edge of the desert, which provided a lot of wide-open space, perfect for driving my bike.

"Can I take my bike out, Dad?"

"Sure, Bill. But make sure you drive it on the sidewalk. Don't drive it across the street. *Walk* it across. You're underage and it's against the law for you to drive it in the street. Let me repeat that. DO NOT DRIVE IT ACROSS THE STREET. Got that?"

"I got it. Heard you loud and clear."

"Sometimes I'm not sure you do hear me."

"No, no, this time it's different."

I tapped my head to show him that his message had sunk in. He sighed, shook his head, and went off into the living room to read the paper. I raced out of the house, hopped on my bike, tooled around town, and stayed on the sidewalk as I'd been told.

Until I came to the corner across from that wide-open desert patch.

It couldn't have been more than thirty feet across the street. I slowed down, checked my mirror, and looked both ways. There was no one around. Not a soul. It would take me ten seconds to drive across the street. To get off the bike and walk it across the street was so ridiculous and so uncool. What if Nunez saw me? That would be the end of his giving me advice, and with my new interest in girls, I desperately needed his knowledge.

I looked again. Double-checked. *Triple*-checked. The street corner was like a ghost town. Nobody around for miles.

I lowered my head and gunned the bike.

About halfway across, I heard the siren.

I don't know where Mr. Maul, the chief of police and my baseball coach, was hiding, but his squad car was behind me with lights flashing in less than two seconds.

"Pull over." His voice crackled through a loudspeaker.

I parked my bike at the curb. I looked longingly at the desert in front of me. It was less than ten feet away, but it might as well have been on Mars. Mr. Maul got out of the squad car and strode over to me.

"Hello, Bill."

"Hi, Mr. Maul. Tough loss last night to the Orioles. I thought my homer would be enough to beat them, but the bullpen fell apart on us—"

"Don't you know it's against the law for you to ride your minibike in the street? You're underage."

"I did not know that, but thank you for the warning. From now on, I will *walk* my vehicle across the street."

"Get off. I'm taking you home. Let's get that bike in the trunk."

"Or if it's easier, I'll just walk my bike home. That way you can stay out here and continue your excellent police work catching real criminals, such as murderers and robbers, who threaten our community. I, for one, have learned my lesson. Never happen again, I promise."

"Bill, get in the car."

I'm not sure what Dad thought when he saw the police car pull into our driveway. I know he wasn't exactly delighted when Mr. Maul delivered me to the back door. Dad wasn't a screamer. He was more of an impose-the-punishment-that-fits-the-crime kind of guy. In fact, Dad liked to have me choose my own punishment.

"What do you think is fair, Bill?" he asked after Mr. Maul left and he'd gone on a ten-minute rant about how disappointed he was in me, a tactic that always made me feel worse than a whipping would. I hung my head as I thought through a punishment that would be acceptable to both of us. I toed the floor.

"How about I'm grounded for two weeks and I can't ride my bike for a month?"

"Hmm."

"And no allowance for a month."

"A month?"

"And, okay, I'm grounded for a month, too."

Dad sighed theatrically. "So be it."

It took me until I was a dad myself to realize that my punishments were far worse than anything he would come up with.

P.S. I never rode my minibike in the street again.

17. MARRYING MISS MILLER

One night at dinner, Dad hit us with some big news.

"Pass the potatoes, Bill," he said. Then he added casually, as he scooped some hash browns onto his plate, "There's someone I want you all to meet."

I knew what he meant. The *someone* was a woman. By his tone of voice I could tell that this was somebody special and that he had been spending a lot of quality time with her.

"Who is she?" I asked.

"What is she like?" Janet added.

"Actually, you know her," he said. He paused. "Her name is Mary Miller."

We looked at him blankly.

"I don't know a Mary Miller," I said.

"You know her as *Miss* Miller."

I looked at him in horror. My sister Jenny dropped her fork. "Miss Miller? My first-grade teacher?"

"That's her."

"No wonder you had so many parent-teacher conferences," I said.

"I know this is kind of awkward," Dad said.

"It's not awkward," I said. "It's *weird*."

We were all silent for a long time. Dad absently poked his green beans with his fork. Finally, Jenny broke the ice.

"Miss Miller used to open my milk boxes for me," she said. "I hate those things. I always mess up and open them from the wrong side."

"Here's a tip," I said. "Open them on the side that says OPEN."

"She was in the first grade," Janet said. "She couldn't read yet."

"You're in the fifth grade. When you gonna learn?"

"I like Miss Miller," Jenny said. "She's nice."

"You can call her Mary," Dad said.

Jenny stared him, horrified. "No, I can't," she said. "She's a *teacher*."

It didn't take very long for us to get used to calling Miss Miller Mary, mostly because Mary made it easy for us. She was sweet and good-natured, a good sport, and she fit right in with us. Before we knew it, Dad hit us with another bombshell.

"Kids, Mary and I are getting married."

Actually, that wasn't the bombshell. We all expected that they'd get married. They were inseparable. I don't think they spent the night together, or if they did, I never noticed, but otherwise Mary felt as if she'd already become our unofficial stepmom. We knew they were getting married. It was just a matter of when.

The bombshell was that we weren't invited to the wedding.

"It's not going to be a big deal," Dad explained. "Just a civil ceremony down at the courthouse. Only Mary, me, and a justice of the peace. We're gonna say our vows, sign a couple of papers, and that's it. It'll be boring for you kids. We'll throw a big party later."

"We're not going?" I asked.

"There's no point," Dad said. "You're gonna stay home with Granddad and Grandma."

Now, I admit that I'm not much of a romantic, but I do my best. I send my wife flowers for no reason. I take her out to dinner in the middle of the week. I even try to listen when she's talking. One time I sat through an entire episode of *Grey's Anatomy* when I could've watched a car chase on the local news.

Even I, natural nonromantic and clueless kid, felt that Dad should have had us at his wedding. We wanted to be there. We wanted to share this new beginning with him.

Instead, the day of Dad and Mary's wedding was a day like any other. Nothing much was said at breakfast. Dad checked his watch, downed the rest of his coffee, went into his room, and came out in his best suit and a new tie. Mary drove up in her car. When she got out, she was wearing a new dress, something very elegant but very simple. Classy. Like her. Granddad took a couple of pictures; they kissed us all good-bye and drove down to Winslow Town Hall.

I watched through the window as Dad and Mary drove off to get married. I felt strangely alone, isolated, as if I had been left out of something important. I tried to put myself in Dad's shoes. I knew that for a long time he'd been unhappy. I remembered those nights when I'd lie in bed and hear him crying on the other side of the wall. I was scared and I felt helpless. After he and Mary started getting serious, I felt an enormous shift, not only in Dad but in the energy of our house. It was a feeling of a weight being lifted. Mary added a literal ray of light to our house.

I guess Dad felt that watching him get married to someone other than our mom might upset us. Or . . . I really don't know. I know that he thought he was doing the right thing.

I came away from the window and joined my sisters and grandparents in the kitchen. Grandma was boiling some water for tea. She stood over the stove. She stared off, something clearly on her mind. I was hoping she wasn't thinking about playing the piano and singing when Dad and Mary got home.

"Well, this is it," she said softly. "You know what you have to do now."

"Uh, add a tea bag?"

"I'm talking about when your father comes home."

I was still at a loss. "Throw rice?"

"No, Willy. I mean about Mary."

"What about her?"

"What are you going to call her?"

I shrugged. "Mary? I was going to call her . . . Mary?"

Grandma shook her head. "From now on, you have to call her *Mom*."

"Mom?" I tried that on for size. It didn't quite fit. I already had a mom.

"It was hard enough not calling her Miss Miller," I said.

"It'd mean a lot to your father."

"Mom," I said, trying it on again. Grandma dipped her head and peered at me.

"I guess I could try," I said.

And then for some strange reason, she reached out and hugged me.

18. GOOD 'N' GREASY

Mary did not tiptoe into our family. She didn't take her time, pick her spots, and ease her way in. She got into first gear and hit the ground running. I always admired that about her. Looking back, I know it wasn't easy for her to come into a family with four crazy school-age kids and a husband who was out all day and many nights, doing work that was rewarding but incredibly stressful. Mary slid right in and took over the Mom role in our house seamlessly and with style and grace. Not that there weren't a few speed bumps on the road.

For one, meals. Coordinating the eating habits, tastes, and schedules of six ordinary people is a difficult juggling act. With us, it was like juggling cats. I'm amazed that Mary didn't throw up her hands after the first meal she cooked and run screaming out into the night, never to be seen again. Actually, she almost did.

She went all out that first night. She cooked steaks, mashed potatoes, gravy, and green beans and made an apple pie. But her cooking was only half the problem. First, she had to adjust to our dinner conversation. When your dad's a doctor, basically anything goes. No subject is off-limits, no description too extreme. In other words, our dinner conversation was unbelievably gross. Not to us. We kids were way into it. Thankfully, Dad was one guy who brought his work home with him. We talked about boogers the size of baseballs that had to be pulled out of noses, bones poking out of flesh, sticking up in the weirdest places, blood spurting out of stomachs, ears, and eyeballs, guts poring onto the ER floor, and sores that oozed brown and yellow slime. It was great.

For some reason, Mary found our dinner conversation disgusting. She was from a very prim and proper South Carolina family, and I guess she was used to talking about music or art or politics or something else equally boring because she just didn't get it. I kept waiting for her to jump in, but she didn't. She just sat at the table, her face turning an alarming shade of green.

Suddenly Dad burst out laughing. "Sorry," he said. "I'm laughing because I know what's coming. Or in this case, what *fell out*."

We kids roared. Mary swallowed, then pressed two fingers over her mouth.

"So this guy comes into the ER," Dad said, waving his fork in the air to make his point. "Midforties, I'd say, can't really tell. Big guy. A little bit dim. He had on a vest and one of those wool hunting caps with earflaps, which he refused to take off."

Dad lowered his head and snickered. He held his fork up like a stop sign. His snicker dissolved into a cackle; then his shoulders started shaking.

"This guy gets wheeled right in, ahead of everyone else. A nurse slaps his chart in my hand. I can tell this is serious. 'Gunshot wound,' she says."

"'What happened?' I asked the guy.

"'Uh, I was turkey hunting,' he said. 'It was dark, on account it was *night*?'

"'Yeah, that dark thing can happen at night.'

"'I had me a few beers, not that many, six or seven. We was sitting around the campsite and I heard a noise in the bush up ahead, not ten feet away. Out scoots this huge gobbler. I grabbed my rifle, aimed, and *fired*.'"

Dad paused, then lowered his head and his voice.

"'Only I missed and shot myself in the thigh.'"

I started roaring. "What was he aiming at?"

Dad's shoulders started shaking again. "He said it was *one of them freak hunting accidents.* He was so drunk and so dumb. We fixed him up. He's fine now."

Dad reached for his knife and started sawing through his steak. It was rough going because the steak was caked in grease.

"You should've seen his leg when he came in," Dad said. "The whole thigh was blown apart. It looked like raw hamburger. The insides were oozing out of his pants—"

By now, Mary had one entire palm jammed over her mouth while with her other hand she fanned herself with her napkin. Dad speared a piece of steak and took a bite. He shook his head. "Um um," he said. "Mary, these steaks are great. How'd you get that greasy taste in 'em?"

That did it. Mary bolted from the table. Dad craned his neck, watching her go.

"What'd I say?"

"No idea," I said. "These steaks are perfect, good and greasy, just the way we like 'em."

What I loved about Mary was that she shook off that first night of gross-out dinner conversation and greasy-steak talk and came back for more the very next night. She cooked dinner again, only this time, to my horror, she made Brussels sprouts.

I am not a picky eater. There are only three things I will not eat: liver, okra, and Brussels sprouts. I don't get how anyone can eat them. Some people go nuts over liver and onions. I say, "Here, enjoy, take mine. Just get far away from me." And eating boiled okra, which is how my mom used to make it, is like sticking a ball of snot in your mouth. It feels and tastes like moist, stringy . . . *snot*. The only way I could eat it was to mush it between two pieces of bread and go for the land speed record: Eat it before I could taste it going down.

Brussels sprouts are the worst. What I don't get is why parents make you eat food that disgusts you. Do they get pleasure out of forcing this stuff on us? Do they see us as prisoners of war? Why don't parents say, "You don't like Brussels sprouts? No, of course you don't have to eat them. Here. Have a Milky Way instead"?

When Mary brought an ornate serving bowl filled with steaming Brussels sprouts to the table that second night, I thought I was going to upchuck right there, right into the bowl. Dad caught the look in my eye along with my ghostlike complexion.

"I hope everyone likes Brussels sprouts," Mary said, smiling.

"We love 'em," Dad said. I could feel his eyes on me like two lasers.

"My . . . favorite," I squeaked.

Dad took a few Brussels sprouts and passed the bowl down the line, from Janet to Judy to Jenny to me. I put one Brussels sprout on my plate and handed the bowl to Mary.

"Just one?" She looked offended.

"Is that all I took? I couldn't see. I must've lost that sprout in the lights."

I dumped two more Brussels sprouts onto my plate, looked down at them, three little green turd balls, and gagged.

"Um umm," Dad said, plowing through his mound of Brussels sprouts as if they were ice cream. "How did you make these?"

"No special way," Mary said. "Just boiled 'em. Same way I make okra."

I really thought I was going to hurl.

"Eat 'em, Bill. They're great. Very tender."

"I'm actually kind of full. But everything was so delicious. May I be excused?"

"Just eat one. Then you can be excused."

Dad looked over at Mary for approval. She nodded, then smiled at me.

It was now or never. I had to come up with a strategy to finish off this one Brussels sprout right now. I knew there was no way I could chew the thing. If I chewed it, it was coming right back up. I had only one choice: Drink a glass of milk and swallow the sprout whole.

I started chugging the milk. I jabbed the Brussels sprout with my fork, popped it into my mouth, and swallowed.

Unfortunately, it came right back up. With the milk. What happened next is too disgusting for even our dinner conversation. I'll just say that bowls, plates, the tablecloth, and a vase full of flowers were involved.

Later, when I was lying in bed in a fetal position, my stomach twisted into knots over the Brussels sprout incident, Mary came into my room.

"How you feeling?"

"I'll live. I think."

Mary brushed her hand in front of her face as if she was swatting away a fly. "You know, Bill, I wish you'd told me that you didn't care for Brussels sprouts."

"That would have been a lie. I don't care for Biff Rankin, the kid who sits behind me and makes farting noises from his armpits. I *hate* Brussels sprouts."

"That's pretty clear to me now."

"I'm sorry about tonight."

"I'm the one who should be sorry. If I knew you hated Brussels sprouts, I never would've made them. I certainly never would've made you *eat* them."

"What? Are you serious?"

"Of course. What parent would make their child eat something they hate?" Mary smiled. "So next time, tell me when you don't like something, okay?"

I smiled back. "Okay." Then I added, quietly, "Mom."

19. GOING TO THE DRIVE-IN

Once Mary settled in, everything in our family settled down. Mom had relocated to Flagstaff and started a new life. She called us often, and every few months my sisters and I would ride the train to Flagstaff and visit her. It was never enough, but at least it was something and the best we could all do. But through late elementary school and junior high, I spent most of my days in Winslow, enjoying an adolescence as normal as every other American kid's.

I was your dream child, the good kid who by the time he was thirteen had every parent's dream résumé: Little League All-Star and Home Run Champion; Cub Scout with so many merit badges I had to pin some on the *back* of my uniform; 4-H Club member (I unfortunately did not participate in raising, caring for, milking, and selling Henrietta, our prize heifer; I was on a different team, whose heifer, Pauline, one night succumbed to the charms of Klondike, the studly local bull who knocked her up and knocked us out of the competition); church choir soloist (yeah, that went *well;* most people thankfully avoided mentioning that my voice roller-coastered from a soprano to a bass and back up again right in the middle of "Amazing Grace" and instead complimented my poise, my suit, or my *haircut*). My parents had a lot to brag about. Through eighth grade I had accumulated zero jail time, and Dad never once mentioned shipping me off to military school.

One of the reasons I stayed out of trouble was that I actually liked hanging out with my family. My sisters and I always got along and got even closer after the divorce. My stepmom and I were friends from the beginning, and after a short while I thought of her as my second mom.

Of course, Dad and I had always been tight. Since the time I was old enough to walk he'd taken me everywhere, from the ER to house calls to fishing and hunting trips. And Dad had a talent for building things. I swear, if he'd ever decided to quit being a doctor, he could've made a living as a carpenter or even a contractor. He was that handy. He built his own barn, from scratch. I was his trusty assistant during most of his projects, except while he was measuring and sawing and hammering, I was catching rays and trying to look busy by pounding in the occasional nail. Mostly I was bored. I loved the hanging out with Dad part. It was the actual working part that I didn't love so much. He'd nurse a beer or two during an entire day of building while I'd pound four or five sodas. He'd sweat and swear, and I'd say, "Dad, you know you can always hire people to do this." He'd grunt and keep on going. I guess I learned some stuff through just watching him, because I turned out to be fairly handy myself. Some things are in the genes.

Next to playing baseball, my favorite activity was going to the movies. In fact, I became kind of a movie nut. I'd go to the Winslow Theater every week, usually Friday night when the new movie came in. If I liked it, I'd go again on Saturday.

One of the first movies I saw was *Oliver!* We drove to Phoenix because Dad wanted to catch it the first night on a huge horseshoe-shaped screen with extra-special color and extra-terrific sound. I was in third or fourth grade, and my first reaction was to cover my ears.

I don't remember much about the movie except that it was about a bunch of poor, hungry English kids and this bad guy named Fagin, and we sat and sat and sat watching this thing for what seemed like *days*. I was bored out of my mind. I kept thinking, *Is this thing ever gonna end? The kid wants a little more slop. Can't you hear him? He wants* more. *Give him more*, please, *so we can get outta here*.

Another movie we went to as a family was *Rosemary's Baby*. My dad had no clue what it was about. I think he figured it was about a family with a mischievous baby who got into a lot of funny high-jinks. We quickly learned that *Rosemary's Baby* was not only scary, it was very risqué. Rosemary gets it on with the *Devil*, for cryin' out loud. Excellent. But perhaps not the perfect choice for a family with young kids. I was *into* this movie, though. This was more like it. I settled back with my popcorn.

The next thing I knew Dad was hustling us out of the theater. We hadn't made it through the first half hour.

"Where we goin'?" I said, clinging to my half-eaten bucket of popcorn.

"Home," Dad said.

"Why? This move was actually good. This isn't fair. I sat all the way through *Oliver!* Let's go back. I wanna pray for *Rosemary's Baby*."

The most fun I had at the movies was at the Winslow Drive-In. When I was growing up, in the 1960s and '70s, the drive-in was known mainly for making out, not watching the movie. I never got to go to the drive-in with a girl. I went with my dad. We used to go at least once a week, because most of the time the drive-in showed an action movie or horror movie, the kind of films designed to frighten women so their dates could comfort them in the backseat.

The first movie I remember going to at the drive-in was a horror film called *The Worms*. The plot is a classic. A swarm of flesh-eating worms lives inside the people of a small town. In the middle of the night, they start eating their way out of their hosts' bodies, boring their way through stomachs, ears, and eyes, crawling through old ladies' hair and coming out of the town gossip's mouth. Eventually the worms eat through everybody in town. The movie ends with the worms crawling toward the next town, presumably on their way to take over the world.

As great as this movie was, it only ranks as my second all-time favorite film.

My number one film is a tie among every film starring John Wayne.

You know the expression "God made man in his own image"?

I know who he had in mind: John Wayne.

I don't remember the first John Wayne movie I saw, but I know I saw it at the drive-in with Dad. I think it was probably *The Man Who Shot Liberty Valance.* I know that for a while, Duke starred in at least one movie a year and I saw them all, not once, but a million times: *McLintock!, In Harm's Way, The Sons of Katie Elder, Cast a Giant Shadow, El Dorado, The War Wagon, Hellfighters, The Undefeated, Chisum,* and, of course, *True Grit,* which finally earned Duke his richly deserved Academy Award.

I'd like to say that John Wayne was my role model, but that doesn't do my feelings about him justice. Truth is, I became a mini John Wayne. I started to walk like him, slowly, deliberately, with a hitch in my step, as if I owned any room I entered. I started to talk like him, too. I copied his speech pattern, aped his rhythm and inflection, and tried to add his tone and timbre.

Most of all, I tried to incorporate his cool.

To me, that's what John Wayne embodied: cool. He never shouted, never flew off the handle, never fumbled with his words. He always knew exactly what to say and when to say it. Of course, I was young and I assumed that actors made up their own lines on the spot. They do, don't they?

Even when he let his fists or his gun do his talking, John Wayne punched or shot with total cool. And his cool was different than James Dean's or Marlon Brando's cool. They were rebellious, young, anti-establishment. John Wayne's cool was a man's cool. There was nothing brash about him. He was just confident. In charge. The Man.

I admit it. When I was a kid, I wanted to grow up to be John Wayne.

Here's the sad part.

I still do.

20. LEAVING ARIZONA

All good things come to an end.

After ninth grade, Dad sold our house in Winslow and we moved to Dallas, where I started high school. I went from a school that had a total of three hundred kids to a *class* of fifteen hundred. Talk about culture shock. I left a town where everybody knew my name to a place where nobody knew I existed.

If it were up to me, I would have stayed in Winslow forever, but parenting was different then. Your parents told you what decision they'd made and all you could do was deal with it.

Today parents include their kids in their decisions, as if they were partners.

"Tommy, Janie . . . Mommy and I are thinking of moving to another city far away. How would you feel about that?"

"I'll miss my friends. I'm not going."

"Me either. I hate you."

"What if moving means we'd live in a larger house, you'd have your own room and bathroom, and Daddy would have a new job that would bring in thousands and thousands more dollars? And what if we got you a dog?"

"I don't care if you get me a pony. I'm not moving."

"Me either. I hate you."

"Well, okay. I didn't want to be vice president of the company anyway. I'll tell them no. I don't want to upset you. This is a family decision."

A family decision?

In our family, there was no such thing. In fact, when I was a kid, I never heard of a family decision in any family.

The parents made the decisions and the kids went along, like it or not. That's what being a kid was: living a life that was totally out of your control and shutting up about it.

We left Winslow on a Sunday. The night before, a whole group of people threw us a good-bye party, a giant outdoor barbecue held in the corral of a friend's ranch. I said good-bye to my friends, my baseball coach, the school principal, my teachers, Richard Nunez, my Cub Scout pack leader, who handed me yet another merit badge, my 4-H Club leader, who gave me a certificate and a gold whistle for some reason, the choir director, who kept saying over and over that my voice would be very difficult to replace, and Natalie, the first girl I ever really kissed, who slipped me a little tongue as a good-bye gift.

We began the drive to Dallas in silence, all of us feeling the loss of Winslow and the nervousness of starting over. In a little while I broke the ice.

"I've heard good things about Dallas," I said.

"What have you heard?" Dad asked.

"You know," I said. "Good things. Very good things. It's *hot*. We will not have to worry about snow."

We cracked up.

The simple fact was, we were moving to Dallas. Period. Done deal. I figured I might as well try to make the best of it, which pretty much sums up my general attitude: "I'm here. Might as well enjoy myself."

Life throws you a lot of curve balls.

You better learn to hit 'em.

21. THE DEATH OF COOL

Arriving in Dallas as a nobody did give me one big advantage in high school: I started off with a clean slate. In Winslow, I was the kid who always came up just short of cool. I'd see a hot girl, hop on my bike, perform an awesome wheelie, come down like a champ, then hit the curb and go sailing over the handlebars. Head bleeding, sirens blaring, ER here I come.

"Hi, Dad."

"Oh, no, Bill, not again. What were you doing, trying to impress some girl?"

"Uh, maybe—"

"Not cool."

In Winslow, I always seemed to end up on the outside of cool, looking in. I walked uncool. The John Wayne hitch I put in my step made me look as if I walked with a groin pull. I dressed uncool. I was thin and wiry and my clothes hung off me. I looked like a human hanger. I even played an uncool instrument in the school band.

I wanted to learn to play trumpet, which was *the* cool instrument, but the band director said that he already had too many trumpet players. Instead, he told me to take up the tuba or the trombone. Since the tuba is the dorkiest instrument ever invented, I went for the trombone— but trust me, there is nothing less cool than riding your bike with a trombone strapped to the back of it. Looks like wings.

In Dallas, to my surprise, I found out that playing the trombone *was* cool. Because not only did I make it into the marching band with my "t-bone," I also got into the jazz band. In my new high school, only the ultra-cool kids got into the jazz band. I went from being just short of cool in Winslow to being genuinely cool in Dallas. Within a couple of months, I also got my driver's license, which changed my life.

To begin with, I didn't have to strap my trombone to the back of my bike with a bungee cord anymore. I stuffed my 'bone into the trunk and *drove* to jazz band practice. Cool.

Just having a license made me cool. At least when I went out on a date, my dad didn't have to drive us. Which is what had happened on my first real date.

I had the hots for a girl named Jeri Gleam, who on the high school scale of ten was an eleven. One day during math class, I got up my courage and asked her to a school dance. To my shock, she said yes.

Since I'm a guy and therefore don't think things through, I hadn't worked out the details of the date.

"How're you and Jeri getting to the dance?" Dad asked.

"Huh. Good question. I haven't thought about it."

"I have. I'll drive you. Take you home, too."

The night of the dance, Dad drove Jeri and me to the high school in our station wagon. We sat in the backseat, pressed against opposite windows, not saying a word. For the occasion, Dad had put on a suit and tie. I think he was pretending to be our chauffeur. He actually looked more like an undertaker. I sure felt like I was sitting in a hearse.

He parked a block from school. Jeri and I hustled out of the station wagon as fast as we could and went into the school gym. The dance turned out great. Jeri and I spent the whole night laughing and flirting. We threw ourselves into all the new dance crazes, came in third in a Twist contest, and, best of all, danced the last dance of the night, a slow one, with our arms around each other. When the dance was over, I did what every kid without a driver's license had to do: I called my dad from a pay phone.

Dad arrived outside the school a few minutes later in the station wagon. He'd changed out of his suit and tie and into a T-shirt and Bermuda shorts. He looked like a tourist on vacation in Disney World. Jeri and I scrambled into the backseat, but instead of hugging the opposite doors, we sat next to each other, holding hands.

Sitting in the backseat, I silently planned my move. Jeri and I had hit it off, that was obvious. I was fairly certain that I was a strong candidate for a long, slow, good-night kiss. There was only one slight problem.

Dad.

He drove about two miles an hour, whistling to a country music station, adjusting the rearview mirror so he could get a better look at us. And that outfit. He'd gone from elegantly dressed chauffeur to dorky-looking chaperone.

Still, I liked my chances. Dad had once been a sophomore in high school himself. He knew how embarrassing it was having your dad drive you and your date home from a dance, especially a date as adorable as Jeri Gleam. Dad was cool. He'd let us out and then drive around the block, slowly, giving us plenty of time to say our proper good nights at her door.

He pulled up in front of Jeri's house.

"Thank you, Dr. Engvall," Jeri said.

"The pleasure was all mine."

"Urmph," I mumbled.

I got out and opened the door for Jeri. We walked up to her front door, then glanced back at the street. Dad waved.

And stayed there.

Parked right in front of her house.

He sat in the front seat, drumming his fingers on the steering wheel, impatient as a getaway driver. Jeri and I stood at her front door in silence, not knowing what to do, but knowing that we really couldn't do anything.

Thanks, Dad, I thought. *Thanks a bunch.*

"I had a nice time," Jeri said.

"Me, too."

"Well," Jeri said.

"Yeah," I said.

Simultaneously, we swiveled our heads toward the station wagon idling at the curb. Yep. He was still there. We turned back toward each other and nearly clunked heads.

"So I guess I'll see you in math," Jeri said.

"Not unless I see you first," I said, and immediately cringed, realizing how lame I sounded.

"Thanks again," Jeri said, and pecked me on the cheek like I was her grandpa.

"Nice kid," Dad said after I got in the car and he pulled away from Jeri's house. "Any time you want to go out with her, let me know and I'll drive you."

"Terrific," I said, knowing that the news of Dad wearing his T-shirt and Bermudas, sitting in our station wagon while we said good night at her front door, was beginning to spread through the high school at that very moment, taking with it my last remnants of cool.

22. I SHOT THE SHERIFF

In high school, my favorite class was creative writing. To be honest, the only reason I took the class was that I had a crush on the teacher.

Her name was Bobbie Brown. She was my Mrs. Robinson. Of course, nothing ever happened between us, except in my imagination. I used to fantasize that Bobbie Brown and I would sneak away during lunch and duck into the custodian's closet together. Kind of embarrassing that the best I could come up with involved me, her, and a janitor's pail. Talk about a lame fantasy.

Although I took her class for the wrong reason—so I could spend an hour a day staring at her—Bobbie Brown was instrumental in getting me to open up creatively. Every couple of weeks she would give us an assignment, offering us a choice of writing a paper or doing a skit. I always chose the skit. I never would've thought that after my first one, my skits would become sort of legendary, and I would eventually perform them in the auditorium in front of the whole school.

Thanks to my stepmom, I'd actually gotten interested in creative writing a few years before in Winslow, at the dinner table. Mary, a former teacher herself, was always looking to help my sisters and me improve academically. She was very creative and avoided rote learning like flash cards or math drills. She went for the more unconventional, fun approach.

One night at dinner, she announced that every Wednesday from then on would be "Writing Night." All of us, even Jenny, who could barely write, would be responsible for reading something that we'd written that week. It could be a story, a poem, a skit, anything. It just had to be short and it had to be original.

My first reaction, which I muttered to myself, was, "What a royal pain in the butt."

Later, when we were all sitting around in her room, Janet said, "I already go to school. Why do we have to go to school at home?"

"This sucks," I said. "I'm not writing *nothin'*."

"Yes, you are."

Dad.

Standing in the doorway. Arms folded, crooked grin on his face, spearing me with his steel-eyed stare that said, without words, "Writing Night is nonnegotiable."

"You didn't let me finish," I said. "I'm not writing nothin' *tonight*. I have too much homework. Homework first, right? Gonna write mine tomorrow."

"I'm gonna write mine tonight," he said.

"You have to do it, too?" I said.

"I don't *have* to, but we're all doing this as a family."

He smiled thinly and left us four kids in silence.

"It might be fun," Janet said after a while.

"It might," I said. "And you might not be ugly."

I ducked the pillow she threw at me and left.

Shocker: Janet was right. Writing Night actually was fun. Dad led off the first night with a funny story about something that had happened in the ER. Mary read a poem. Janet, Judy, and Jenny acted out a short skit they'd written.

I read a weird short story I'd written inspired by my favorite TV show at the time, *The Twilight Zone.* In my story, a guy is on a plane, minding his own business, reading a newspaper. The passenger next to him gets up and goes to the bathroom. Suddenly, a little girl appears and sits down in the vacant seat next to him. She tells him that the plane is going to crash, then, poof, she's gone, vanished into thin air. The guy gets up and tries to warn the pilot, but the flight attendant stops him. He tries to warn the other passengers, but nobody believes him. He starts to panic. He gets so nuts that all the people around him have to restrain him. Then he wakes up. He feels incredibly relieved that this has all been a dream. He grabs his newspaper and starts to read. The passenger sitting next to him gets up to go to the bathroom. He feels a presence standing over him. It's the little girl.

"Is this seat taken?" she says.

As I read, I could sense that my entire family had gotten caught up in the story. I felt something else, too, something I had never felt before.

A kind of power.

I had total command of this audience. True, it was a small, supportive, and captive audience, but they were hanging on my every word. They were riveted.

I loved having their attention focused on me. This wasn't about my ego. Well, maybe a little bit, but mainly I loved that I could actually entertain them.

What was truly amazing was that it felt effortless.

It felt natural—writing something, performing it in front of an audience, and connecting to an audience. All of it. It felt *right,* almost as if it were meant to be.

The first skit I wrote and performed in Bobbie Brown's creative writing class was about a sheriff in a small western town. Although inspired by my love of western movies and John Wayne, this sheriff was nothing like the Duke. He was a pompous, clumsy, clueless idiot. I also tried something different. Unlike the stories and skits I'd written for Writing Night, this skit had no dialogue, no words. It was a silent sketch, a pantomime, the only sound coming from a tape I'd made.

I threw myself into this project. Well, so did my dad. We built scenery and props, and I designed and wore a costume. The centerpiece of the skit was my horse. We constructed a nearly life-sized horse out of a fifty-gallon drum. I found a horse's head in a magazine, blew it up, and cut it out. Dad and I built four legs and a tail, and then I nailed all of the body parts onto the drum. Then I hitched a saddle over it. Finally, we rigged the horse's hind legs so that when I pulled a hidden string, the legs kicked.

Building the horse was one thing; getting it to school was another. Fortunately, I had just gotten my driver's license. Promising that I would keep my eyes focused on the road and off any pretty girls and that I would drive under the speed limit, I convinced my dad to loan me his cherished El Camino. I loaded the horse into the back of the El Camino and slowly and carefully drove to school. I did get my share of looks on the way. Some were directed to the horse in the back; some were directed toward me because I was dressed in full sheriff costume.

It turned out that the horse was too big to fit in the classroom, so I had to perform my skit outside, between buildings. As I set up, Bobbie

Brown moved the entire bewildered class to my open-air performance space. They all laughed when they saw me in costume standing by my horse. Staying in character, I just stared pompously at them, playing it straight.

I started the skit sitting at my desk, admiring myself in a mirror. I combed my hair. Slicked back the sides with saliva. Raised my eyebrows. Slicked them back with saliva, too. Satisfied, I smiled at myself. Posed. Turned this way and that. *Man, I'm a great-looking sheriff.*

Suddenly there were gunshots, which I'd prerecorded on a portable tape deck I'd stuck under the desk. I raced out of my imaginary office, drew my gun, and started shooting at outlaws in the distance. They shot back. I ducked, ran toward my horse, dropped my gun, and reached down to get it. I then pulled the hidden string. The horse's hind legs shot out and kicked me in the head. I fell over, tumbling over into a somersault. I picked myself up, ran to the horse, and leaped on. I had purposely put the saddle on loosely, and as I jumped onto the horse, the saddle flew off.

The rest of the sketch is a blur. I just know that whatever I did got drowned out by the class's hysterical laughter and then by their applause. I bowed slightly and smiled, and still the class clapped and cheered.

I couldn't articulate it then, but somehow I knew that making people laugh was my calling—and that someday it was going to be my career.

23. THE THIRTY-MINUTE RULE

In high school, I was a late bloomer. I started shaving second semester sophomore year. I shaved again first semester junior year. I watched enviously as most of the guys in my class enjoyed growth spurts everywhere on their bodies. I, on the other hand, was the king of the land called arrested development. Nothing grew at the pace I wanted it to. I watched with awe as some kids shaved with an electric razor in the bathroom between periods. One guy, Ronnie Van, had just turned sixteen but looked about forty. He had five o'clock shadow at nine o'clock in the morning. He had a voice as deep as the lead singer in the Temptations. The girls loved him.

I looked and sounded like Opie.

To compensate for being a late bloomer, and because I needed money, I decided to get a job.

Junior year, after a short time pounding the pavement, I landed my first job ever: dishwasher at Guido's Delicatessen. Not exactly my dream job. In fact, if I judged all future jobs by this one, I might never have worked again.

My dishwasher's duties were simple: I had to collect plates of left-over scrambled eggs, half-eaten pancakes, gooey omelet remains, and stinky slabs of various types of mystery meat, spray these plates with a high-pressure hose that shot out water that was about a million de-grees, and then scrub the plates spotless. Guido was such a tyrant that I often wanted to blast him with the hose. I wore latex gloves up to my elbows and a baseball cap turned backward, and for some reason Guido insisted that I wear an apron.

"You in kitchen, you wear apron!" he shouted.

"Why? I'm a dishwasher, not a cook."

"It's the law!"

"What law?"

"Guido's Law!"

There were times, like every five minutes, that I wanted to rip off my apron, roll it into a ball, and shove it up Guido's nose. But I stayed and worked hard, without complaining. For one thing, Guido, despite being an A-hole, paid well. Second, since this was my first job, I figured all bosses were A-holes. I didn't know any better. I learned later that most bosses, like most people, are actually okay. Plus, as I said, my nature is to hang in there and make the best of things. So I did. I blasted away with my hose, scraped off the dirty dishes from the morning rush with my gloves, and blocked out Guido as he screamed and cursed at customers and employees equally in his broken English.

Six months later my job crashed and burned.

"Guido, can I talk to you for a minute?"

"I no give you a raise. Fuggetaboutit."

"I'm not asking for a raise. You're more than generous."

"Why you kiss my ass? What you want?"

"I need to take Saturday night off. It's my high school prom."

"You want off for *prom*?"

"Please."

"No."

"No?"

"You deaf? NO."

"It's my prom," I said again.

"I heard. BFD. Answer is *no*. Now wash."

"Guido, I'm going to the prom. I already got a date, bought the tickets, rented a tux, got her a corsage—"

He shrugged. "You waste lotta money buying all that crap."

"I'll make up the hours."

"You make up nothin'. Because you gonna work."

"I'm going to the prom," I said, no longer caring where this was headed.

"You forget Guido's Law," Guido said.

"Another law? What's this one?"

"No Prom Law. You go to prom, you fired."

"Too late," I said.

"Hah?"

"I *quit.*"

I flung off my apron, rolled it into a ball, and stuffed it into the sea of soapy water in the sink.

"You owe me for apron!" he shouted.

"Shove it up your—"

The sound of the door slamming as I stormed out drowned out the rest of my sentence.

I went to the prom, feeling a huge amount of relief. I'd quit my first job, but I'd stood up to Guido and I felt great.

As far as my next job went, I stayed in the area of working with water. I soon got hired as a lifeguard at a city pool, a job I stayed at through the rest of high school and most of college. It was a perfect job for me: sitting out in the sun catching rays, watching little kids frolic in the shallow end, and, best of all, flirting with their cute babysitters.

B y the beginning of senior year, I was able to afford my own car. I bought a beauty, a used 1962 blue Ford Falcon. It drove like a dream. Didn't matter that it burned a quart of oil about every twenty miles. It was mine. All mine. Cost me a hundred bucks, so you bet I took care of my baby.

I felt like a king driving my Falcon—but I wanted to soup it up, customize it so it would appeal to girls. First move: I took out all the mats and replaced them with inch-thick blue shag carpeting. I realize now that the car probably looked like it belonged to a pimp, but when I was in high school, I thought that the way to a girl's heart was through wall-to-wall carpeting. Even in a car.

That's what life was about in high school. Girls. I had entered a new phase. I liked them. A lot. I liked to talk to them, hold hands with them, flirt with them, and I *loved* to kiss them. I never went any farther than kissing because (a) I was a good, moral, churchgoing kid and (b) they wouldn't let me.

No question about it, the Falcon gave my social life a boost. Dad was now officially canned as chauffeur and chaperone. That was a plus right there.

Most of my dates followed the same familiar pattern. I'd pick the girl up, engage in small talk with her parents, charm the mom, and assure the dad that we'd be home by eleven. We'd get into the Falcon, the girl would snuggle close, and comment on the cushiness of the carpet, and then and we'd go to a movie and maybe get a bite to eat. Afterward I'd drive her home and we'd park in front of her house, where we'd make out in the front seat like a couple of wild overheated sex-starved teenagers, which, come to think of it, we were. Finally, my date would break away, say good night, and hop out of the car. I'd start up the car, pull away from the curb, and crash into something.

It was uncanny. I'd get so worked up kissing that when I started driving, I wouldn't look where I was going. I couldn't. I didn't have control. It was like I was driving through a haze.

It was really bad the first time this happened because I didn't know the effect kissing had on me. I was blindsided, caught completely off guard. It was as if someone had slipped a drug into my drink.

What was even worse was that the girl I was dating lived down the block from me. We pulled up in front of her house, we kissed like crazy, she got out, and I drove off. I was so excited that I never bothered to check my mirror as I pulled away. I never saw the woman coming down the street in her brand-new Pontiac. So brand-new that she still had paper license plates. I plowed right into her. The fender of the Falcon didn't just smash into the side of her car, it took a divot.

"My baby!" the woman screamed, loud enough to jolt me out of my make-out stupor.

She pulled over, examined the gorge my car had ripped out of the side of her car, and slumped against the passenger door. I thought she was going to pass out.

"Didn't you see me?" She spoke just above a whisper.

"Well, uh, no."

"You have to *look,*" she said, her voice rising. "What's the matter with you?"

I considered trying to explain that I had just been kissing a girl and that had rendered me useless, groggy, and virtually incapacitated and that I hadn't known this would be the result of driving immediately after making out. This was my first time driving under the influence of kissing. She was my unfortunate first victim.

"My car isn't even a week old," the woman moaned miserably.

"It's not that bad," I said. "All you gotta do is pound out the gash with a sledgehammer. First, though, you'd have to melt down the dents with a blowtorch—"

She started to cry.

"I'm sorry," I said. "Please don't cry."

She blubbered even more. I sighed, bent down and studied the damage once again.

Amazing, I thought. *Her car is torn to crap and my Falcon doesn't even have a scratch. I wonder how much she paid for her Pontiac. I paid a hundred dollars for my baby.*

Right then I decided that there should be a cooling-off period after I kissed a girl. A minimum of half an hour. That seemed about the proper amount of time needed for my heart rate to return to normal, and for me to regain control of my faculties. Thirty minutes. The minimum amount needed for my vision to clear and for the mushiness to disappear from my brain.

It was like the no-swimming rule. You can't go swimming for thirty minutes after you eat. I could not drive a car until thirty minutes after I kissed a girl.

From that moment on, I decided to instate the Thirty-Minute Rule whenever I or any of my friends went out on a date. It became my mission in life to keep all recently kissed teenaged boys off the streets. Thirty minutes can save a life. I would live by my rule, and I wanted my friends to intervene in the event that I slipped.

"Bill, I saw you kissing a girl."

Sigh. "Okay, you got me."

"Give me your keys."

Resigned. "Here. Take 'em."

"I'll let you know when thirty minutes have passed."

"Thanks, buddy. You know I'd do the same for you."

"I know. By the way, did that carpeting come standard with your car? Because if it did, I'm buying me a Falcon."

24. COLLEGE DAZE

With the end of my senior year of high school hurtling toward me at breakneck speed, Dad and I sat down to discuss my future.

This wasn't my idea. In fact, I spent most of senior year ducking Dad and avoiding this conversation. A lot of great things had happened to me senior year: I'd suddenly shot up, getting some height, which forced me to give up my elf status; I'd become a stellar member of the swim team, discovering that running around poolside in my Speedo with my new height was an excellent way to meet girls; I'd performed mightily in the jazz band, learning that playing sultry jazz with a moody expression and sunglasses was an excellent way to meet girls. I was meeting a lot of girls. Senior year rocked!

I also made some great friends. My best friend from junior year on was my buddy Rick, the most laid-back, hang-loose dude who'd ever come through the state of Texas. Rick's attitude toward life, no matter what was going on, could be summed up in one word: "Whatever."

But when I saw Dad coming toward me with that look on his face, the one that said, "Son, we've got to talk," I picked up my pace, threw it in third gear, and tried to hit the road.

"Bill! Where you going?"

"Band practice, Dad. Love to chat. Gotta run."

"We need to have a conversation. And we're gonna have it right now."

"Uh . . . about what?"

"Your future. Bill, you're gonna be graduating soon. We have to talk about college."

Dad had hit a nerve. I knew I was facing a couple of minor obstacles when it came to graduating high school and going to college, namely graduating high school and getting *into* college. It's not that my grades were bad. Well, okay, they were. I remember showing my report card to Rick one day.

"Man," he said, "your grades suck."

"My dad wants to talk to me about college. What am I gonna do?"

"College? With these grades, that's a long shot. Hey, I have an idea."

"What?"

"Let's go to the drive-in. Double feature. *Women in Chains* and *Prison Break Hotties.*"

"Cool. I'll drive."

Somehow I managed to avoid having the "talk" with Dad. I figured that I'd somehow squeak by and graduate, and then I'd bite the bullet and enroll in one of those trade schools where all the kids wore helmets, but Dad surprised me. He had me fill out an application to Southwestern University, a small, private Methodist university, which happened to be his alma mater. It's also a very good school, which made it even more amazing that I got in. I figured Dad must've bought them a building.

What made my future seem even brighter was that Rick got into Southwestern, too. I'll never forget Rick's reaction when I told him we'd be going off to college together, the Terrible Twosome.

"You got into Southwestern? What'd your dad do, buy them a building?"

To be honest, I wasn't sure I was college material. I decided to hold off my final decision until I visited the college for a Pre-Frosh Weekend. Driving to campus, Rick made sure I understood the main rules about college life.

"You know, Engvall, they don't take roll."

"What?"

"They don't care if you show up for class or not. Dude, it's *college*. You come and go as you please."

"I think you just changed my life."

The Pre-Frosh Weekend sealed the deal. We arrived on campus Friday just after lunch. It was a hot late-spring day and everybody was outside. The guys were throwing Frisbees; the girls were sunbathing on the lawn. It seemed like one big party. It also seemed that if I'd didn't step carefully, I'd trip over yet another beautiful college coed in a bikini.

"I like this place," I said to Rick. "It's very educational."

We were put up in a freshman dorm. Within minutes we were invited to a fraternity party, which lasted from about eight o'clock Friday night until sometime Sunday morning. Everywhere I turned there was a keg of beer and a dozen gorgeous sorority girls.

"Do these girls really go here or were they brought in just for this weekend?" I asked Rick.

"I don't know," said Rick, pouring himself the first of what would be a million beers, "and I don't care."

By midnight, we were obliterated. We danced to "Louie, Louie," played hockey with brooms and rolled-up socks, and at 3:00 A.M. went on a road trip with a couple of blond sorority girls. We somehow found ourselves at the athletic center, where we sneaked into the campus pool. We climbed the pool fence, took off our clothes, and dove in. There is nothing like skinny-dipping with new friends. You haven't lived until you've jumped naked off the high board with a beautiful blonde.

"What year are you guys?" my blonde asked.

"Seniors," Rick said.

"Cool," Rick's blonde said.

"In high school," I said.

There was a pause.

"*Cool,*" Rick's blonde said.

"Cannonball!" my blonde said, pulling me out of the pool and back up to the high board.

And I thought I wasn't college material? Wronggg!

25. BURNING DOWN THE HOUSE

In college I made up for lost time. I was such a good kid in high school that once I became a college freshman, I let loose. I joined a fraternity as soon as they let me. I knew that the center of college social life happened on Fraternity Row. I needed to be a main part of that. There was also something more.

After you get through the crap of pledging, hazing, and Hell Week, you are inducted into a new family. You officially become a *brother*. Family has always been the most important element of my life, even during college, even if my family was one that centered on drinking rivers of beer, chasing half-naked college girls, and playing rock music loud enough to shatter the eardrums of dogs. It was still a family.

I admit it. I didn't really apply myself much to my studies. In order to do that, I would've had to go to class and occasionally open a book. Attending class, studying, taking exams—all that stuff seriously got in the way of the main point of college: partying. Plus a couple of other important activities.

Like intramural tackle football.

Southwestern was supposedly one of only two colleges in the country that still allowed full contact intramural football. With pads, of course. Our fraternity took football seriously. We were campus champs two years running. Our secret? We didn't believe in training. Why leave your game on the practice field? Save it for Saturday afternoon. Come Saturday we'd drink a few beers, put on our pads, and go out there and try to kill somebody. It was great. We attracted huge crowds. I tore up my shoulder a couple of times, but in my beery, bleary-eyed condition I felt nothing.

At our fraternity football games, everyone was drunk: players, fans, referees. Nobody knew what was going on. We'd lose track of time, the number of the down, the score. Minor things. But we were deadly serious about winning.

One time, I tackled a huge behemoth of a guy. The moment I rammed into him I felt something tear in my shoulder. It was a beautiful hit, hard and clean. The crowd went wild. For a moment, the cheering of the crowd drowned out the throbbing in my shoulder. I tried to get up, but pain shot through me and I slumped into a heap at midfield. A bunch of my fraternity brothers ran toward me, along with one premed student, the trainer, who was so drunk he tripped over a hash mark. Someone handed me a beer. Then they slid me onto a stretcher and carried me off the field to a roar from the crowd. I sat up, waved with my good arm, and started screaming obscenities at the other team. I shouted at them the whole way to the medical center, where I passed out from the combination of pain and beer.

One of my downfalls was my roommate: Rick. The two of us became the poster boys for insanity. If we'd spent half the time going to class and studying that we did sleeping, drinking, and partying, we'd have graduated with distinction. Well, we would have *graduated.*

For some reason, probably because we were all drunk, we voted Rick the House Safety Chairman. That's like electing Britney Spears Mother of the Year. It's not that Rick was *against* safety. It's just that his "whatever" attitude didn't quite fit with the demands of his position.

One night we were having a chapter meeting. We were engaged in a very intense discussion over where to put the new pool table we'd just purchased. Some of the brothers wanted it in the living room; others said it belonged in the basement rec room. The discussion became very animated and very personal. Suggestions about where one might insert a pool cue abounded. At one point, Rick excused himself and went upstairs. He came down a few minutes later and said casually, "Uh, guys, I know we have to make a decision on the pool table, but the house is on fire."

We all looked at him as if he'd spoken in a foreign language. I finally broke the ice. *"What?"*

"Yeah. There's flames everywhere. I went up to smoke a cigarette. I flicked my match into the ashtray, only I missed and the match landed on the carpet. It's amazing how fast shag carpeting can burn. Wow. You think I'm a pyro?"

"Call 911!" someone yelled.

"Run!" someone else yelled.

"My bird!" I yelled.

Rick looked at me. "Your what?"

"Petey!" I shouted. "My parakeet!"

Just then a cloud of black smoke billowed down the stairs and engulfed the room. The brothers scattered, pulling off their shirts, covering their mouths and noses. I stood in the middle of the room, still as a statue, tears from the smoke running down my face.

"Don't even think about it," Rick said, grabbing my arm.

I knocked his arm away. "I'm going in," I said. I tore off my shirt and wrapped it over my face like a bank robber.

Rick looked at me with disbelief. "He's a *bird*!"

"Out of my way."

I flew up the stairs two at a time. Smoke poured out of our bedroom, which was at the end of the hallway. My eyes stung. Either by instinct or because of a scene I saw in some movie, I threw myself onto the hallway floor and crawled on my stomach military style toward our room. In the distance I heard sirens wailing. Somebody called my name, shouted for me to come downstairs. My face an inch above the floor, I kept crawling.

I got to our room, stood up, and kicked open the door. I rushed inside.

"Petey! Daddy's here!"

I waved frantically at the smoke. I felt a ball of something hot and heavy fill up my lungs, and I started to cough.

"Petey!" I screamed. "Hang on!"

I reached my desk, where I kept Petey's birdcage. The birdcage was gone. In its place was a tiny mound of melted metal. Petey's ashes lay somewhere in the charred remains of the cage.

"Damn," I said.

For a split second, I thought about gathering what was left of Petey and his cage so I could provide him a proper burial. Our bedroom door burst open and a firefighter rushed in.

"Let's go, buddy," he said. He steered me out of the room, into the hallway, down the burning staircase, through the smoke-filled living room, and out onto the front lawn, where a crowd of over a hundred people had gathered. Rick, a cigarette dangling from his lips, raised his eyebrows and asked, "Well?"

"I was too late," I said.

"I figured," he said. Rick turned to the people clustered behind him. "The bird's fried." He turned back to me and patted me on the back. "Tough break." Rick dropped his cigarette onto the sidewalk and crushed it out with the heel of his boot. "No offense, but remind me to ask you not to save me."

"He was a good bird," I said.

"Yeah. He was great."

I brushed away a tear. "I think he called my name." I choked back a sob. "I heard him say, '*ENG-WAAAAaaaaaa* . . . '"

Rick rolled his eyes and handed me a beer.

We watched the firefighters put out what was left of our room.

26. TEQUILA AND LONGNECKS

The fire department managed to contain the fraternity house fire in record time. The result was minimal damage. Other than barbecuing the hallway and roasting most of the upstairs carpeting, Petey was the biggest casualty. We called an emergency chapter meeting the next night to deal with our safety issue. The first order of business was to remove Rick as House Safety Chairman, for the "good of all mankind."

"It's you guys' fault," Rick said. "I never wanted the job. I was ill suited for the position. Safety is not something I think about much."

"No kidding," the president of the fraternity said.

"He gets distracted," I explained. "Rick should never be allowed anywhere alone, that's all. He needs a spotter. And he should be kept far away from anything flammable."

Everyone agreed. At that point, the fraternity unanimously elected Rick and me Social Chairmen. Our duties and responsibilities were few but critical. We were in charge of parties.

"I think we should have a party Saturday night to celebrate not having our house burn down," Rick said.

"I move we have a Tequila and Longneck Party," I said.

"All those in favor?" Rick said.

"Aye!" everyone shouted.

"It is so decreed," the president said. "Now, I have a question for the co-chairs."

"Shoot."

"What's a Tequila and Longneck Party?"

"I don't know," Rick said. "We just made it up."

In all modesty, inventing a Tequila and Longneck Party on the spot was inspired, if not downright genius. It wasn't often that our fraternity parties had a theme.

"This is awesome, " Rick said as we unfolded the legs on a long banquet table. "Shots of tequila. Lone Star longnecks." Rick shook his head. "We have a gift."

The concept was simple. We'd set up three long banquet tables on which we'd lined up shot glasses of tequila. Under the tables we'd placed several metal tubs full of Lone Star longnecks on ice. The idea was to pound back a shot of tequila, then chase that immediately with a longneck.

"Is this tequila any good?" I asked as Rick poured out the shots.

"Supposed to be."

"Yeah, but how do you *know?* I mean, we are serving it to guests."

"True," Rick said, then paused. "You think we should try it?"

"We're the Social Chairmen. We *have* to try it. It's our responsibility."

"You're right."

Rick poured us each a shot. We clinked glasses. I sipped my tequila, swished it around in my mouth like a fine wine, then chugged it. Rick looked at me. "Well?"

"Not sure."

Rick poured us another shot. This time I pounded back the tequila, opened a bottle of Lone Star, and chugged that.

"I might need one more to be sure."

Four shots of tequila and longnecks later, Rick and I were bombed and the party hadn't even started.

"Here's the thing," Rick said, slurring his words.

"What thing?"

"The thing *is*."

"Yeah?"

"About this party. Somethin' you should know."

"Which is."

"Which *is*." Rick paused. "Carol's coming."

I stared at him. "*Carol's* coming?"

"Yeah. She wants to see if you've changed. See if you've become a little more *serious*."

I started to giggle. Then I started to laugh. Then Rick and I broke into hysterics.

Carol was my old girlfriend. We'd split up, but I was still crazy about her. She'd transferred to another school.

"This ain't good," I said, which caused Rick and me to dissolve into even more hysterics.

"Maybe you should sober up," Rick suggested.

"Why?" I poured myself another shot of tequila. "I'm not drunk."

I chugged the shot, pulled on another longneck, and passed out under the table.

When I came to, the party was in full swing, girls and guys were dancing and hollering, the horns from the band Chicago were wailing over the sound system, and Rick and another guy were dragging me out of the living room.

"Cool. Where we goin'?"

"The shower," Rick said.

"Took a shower three days ago, man."

"Carol's on her way," Rick said. "You don't want her to see you like this."

"I'm fine. Outta my way."

I felt Rick and the other guy slow down, then stop, then I felt their hands under my arms as they stood me up. I squared my shoulders and waved them away. I took one tentative step, then another. "See?"

I took another step. I looked up. My gaze caught something in the ceiling fan. I tilted my head, studied the ceiling. Then the room started to spin. It whirred above me. Spinning, whirling, everything a dizzying, distant blur. I took another step and fell face first into a bowl of guacamole.

Don't remember what happened next. I was standing, I knew that, and water trickled down my face, then the water came in rivulets and drenched me, and then a hard spray swatted me on top of the head. Felt *nice*. The warm, soothing shower spray rained over me—then suddenly ice-cold water daggers stabbed me. I screamed, and then I was awake, but then I slid away, down a chute, and I was in dreamland. I felt myself walking, led into a room, hey, my room, and I saw my bed rising up off the floor, and then, bang, I crash-landed into my pillow.

Good night.

The sunlight pouring in through my window jabbed me awake. I started to sit up. My head began clanging as if someone had inserted a school bell inside one of my eardrums. I fell back down. Somewhere in the distance I heard a large cat purring. More like a rumble than a purr. I took a deep breath and rose up onto my elbows. I surveyed the room. Crunched into the corner of his bed was Rick, out cold, still in his clothes. His mouth was open. It was he who was purring. I yawned and grimaced in pain. My eyebrows hurt.

I looked down at myself. I was under the covers, and I could feel that I was only wearing my boxers.

Then I felt something else, something unnatural, something itchy. I reached down, yanked off the covers, and stared at my body.

I was covered in red.

Blood.

My arms, legs, and chest were streaked in wiggly lines of blood. I was about to scream—and then I realized that it wasn't blood after all.

It was nail polish.

I squinted at my legs and arms and saw that my fraternity brothers had written every curse word you can think of and some you never heard of all over my body.

Then I saw the main attraction.

Across my chest someone had written in large bloodred nail polish: CAROL WAS HERE.

I felt my face flush with embarrassment even though Rick and I were the only ones in the room and Rick was out cold.

Carol was here? I thought. *She saw me like this, passed out, dead to the world, a useless pile of flesh? And then she wrote on my* chest?

I was starting to feel less optimistic about the chances of our getting back together.

Rick rolled over. He scratched his nose in his sleep. His mouth opened like a trap door. He resumed snoring and purring louder than ever.

Then it hit me. I peered at my chest to be sure. Yep. It was unmistakable.

Rick was the one. He'd written "Carol was here" on my chest. I recognized his handwriting.

I sighed, drifted back to sleep.

It wasn't over with Carol.

27. CAVE MAN

It was totally over with Carol.

She got engaged to a guy at her new school, which became a problem in our relationship. Not to mention that I was serial dating myself.

The girls I went out with were all cute and fun, but a couple turned out to be weird. I liked weird. Weird could be sexy. Except sometimes weird could be just *weird*. One girl, Hannah, won the prize for weird going away.

Hannah didn't like to go out to the movies or bowling or to parties. These were too boring, too mundane. Instead, Hannah liked to go to the cemetery near campus and drink cherry vodka on the graves. The first time we did it, I thought it was quirky and cool. Didn't faze me that we were alone in a graveyard, having a picnic at midnight. Well, it fazed me a little. Okay. *It freaked me out.*

"Isn't this great?" she said, sipping her drink from a plastic cup, using a headstone as a coffee table.

"It's awesome." I chugged a beer. I've never been partial to fruity drinks. I looked around the cemetery. An owl hooted. I jumped. Then I felt a chill. I was starting to get spooked. I had to lighten the mood.

"Hannah, you know how many people are dead in here?"

"How many?"

"All of 'em." I waited for her to laugh. Nothing. She didn't react at all, didn't move a muscle. She just stared at the gravestones, off in her own bizarre world.

"Yep," I said aloud. "All these people are dead. I mean, it's fine. Not like they're gonna show up."

I laughed a little too loud. Hannah closed her eyes and muttered something in a language I didn't understand. It sounded like a chant.

"Hey, you know what? I just remembered. I gotta get over to the fraternity. We got a chapter meeting."

She didn't move.

"Hannah? We gotta go."

She still didn't budge. She swayed from side to side locked in some kind of a trance.

"Hannah!" I reached over and touched her arm. She opened her eyes, saw me, and screamed, which caused me to scream. I caught myself, took a deep breath, and spoke in a calm, controlled voice even though I was shivering as if I were standing naked on the North Pole.

"I have to get going," I said gently.

"Why didn't you say so?"

We rolled up the blanket and headed to the car. I led the way in a brisk walk, trying not to break into a run. Didn't look left, didn't look right, kept my eyes forward. Turned on the car and peeled out of there.

Hannah was so cute that she could get me to do almost anything. But drinking on the gravestones? Uh-uh. No way I was going back to the cemetery. Even if it meant sex.

We only went back three more times before I broke up with her for the sake of my sanity.

It didn't take long for me to start feeling guilty about the small fortune my dad was shelling out for my college education. Especially since I was majoring in partying and taking a minor in oversleeping. To ease the guilt, I always had a job.

The jobs weren't much. They paid minimum wage and weren't very exciting. I had to rely on my own creativity and ingenuity to keep me interested.

For a while I worked the night shift for the phone company replacing old telephone wires. That was cool because when I switched the old wires and put in the new ones, I could listen in on conversations. I had to. Otherwise how would I know if the new wiring worked? The conversations I listened to were pretty dull, anyway. Except when I got assigned to rewire one of the girls' dorms. Those conversations got a little more interesting. I especially enjoyed when a girl would be talking to her boyfriend back home, pledging her undying love, and I knew she was lying through her teeth because I'd just seen her running around with my fraternity brother at one of our parties. I was almost tempted to cut in and say, "This is the telephone company. She's lying to you, dude. And lady, you should dump him and go out with me."

I did the phone rewiring job for a few months and then got a job at a one-man gas station. Now, this was a boring job. I would sit in the office for hours with absolutely nothing to do. I was so bored, I started smoking. I know that's not an excuse, but it was either that or do homework. Occasionally, like once an hour, a car would pull up to one of the pumps for gas. I'd hustle out of my little office and offer super service. I'd pump the gas, check the oil and water, wash the windows. I was so bored I would've have washed the whole car and rotated the tires.

My only other diversion was feeding the chickens that belonged to an old farmer who lived in a shack behind the gas station. I'd grab a bag of corn nuts and flick a handful into the driveway. A few would bounce onto the highway. The chickens would go running after the corn nuts, and all of a sudden I'd hear a horn honk and a loud chicken squawk. I'd cringe.

One time, I thought I was going to die at the gas station. It was about eight at night and it was bitter cold. You might not think so, but it actually gets freezing cold in Texas, most commonly when the north winds blow through. The temperature plunges suddenly, violently. It gets so cold the air feels as if it's cutting your face.

I was sitting in the office that night, alone, as usual. "Office" is really too fancy a word; it was more like a closet with four plywood walls. On nights like these, I'd borrow a small space heater from the frat house. That night I cranked the heater up to max. I huddled over it and rubbed my hands together, allowed the heat to circulate. Finally, I leaned back in my chair, lit a cigarette, and took a drag.

I heard the rumble of a truck pulling into the station. I took another drag off my cigarette just as a massive gas truck came to a stop a few feet from the office. The driver climbed out of the cab and started pumping gas from the truck into the holding tank. He saw me inside and nodded. I waved back. No point in my leaving my warm, cozy office. I exhaled a couple of smoke rings off my cig, just to be cool.

Then the hose in the driver's hand somehow ripped in two. A torrent of gas shot up and pelted the office window.

I looked at the gas spraying and soaking the window, the space heater at my feet, the lit cigarette in my fingers, and I freaked. I bolted out of the office, ran across the highway, and dove into a ditch. I got into a fetal position, covered my head with my hands, and waited for the explosion. I closed my eyes and waited. And waited . . .

"You can come out now."

The driver. Arms folded, staring down at me in the ditch. His voice quivered. He was trying hard not to laugh.

"It's safe," he said. "I shut off the gas."

I sat up. "I knew it was safe. I had to jump in here. Part of our training. Like a fire drill."

I climbed out of the ditch and started to cross the street. I stopped, took the pack of cigarettes out of my pocket, crumpled the pack, and tossed it into the ditch. I vowed to give up smoking for the rest of my life. I only recently quit for good after twenty-plus years of trying, but at least I never lit up again near a puddle of gas.

My next job was the one I enjoyed most. I got hired as a tour guide for an underground cave called Inner Space Caverns. I had to wear a jumpsuit and memorize a spiel about stalactites and stalagmites, which I didn't bother to do because it was more fun making the stuff up. Most of the tour groups loved when I ad-libbed. They knew I was putting 'em on and they went along with it. It was cool, kind of like the beginning of my standup. The only problem was when I got stuck with a group of geeky kids who'd actually studied caves and geology. I still faked my way though by changing the subject or telling some story I made up about murderers lurking in the cave. That'd shut 'em up.

My favorite thing to do was to lead a tour group into the center of the cave and turn off all the lights. In my best Bill Nye the Science Guy voice I'd say, "What you're experiencing now is total darkness."

Of course, you also experience total darkness when you close your eyes, but why burst their bubbles?

If I had a good tour group, I'd leave the lights off and sneak away. I carried a flashlight with me, and I'd flick it on and say, "There's a door five hundred yards up to the right if y'all wanna get out. Bye!"

They'd freak out, screaming, "Hey! Hey! Hey! Come back here!"

Man, that was funny. If there happened to be a bunch of geeky science kids in the group, I'd wait a while before I came back, and I'd say, "Thought I saw something up there hiding in the dark. Mighta been one of them murderers."

Getting *paid* to scare people? My dream come true.

28. I WRITE THE SONGS

I led a secret life.

When nobody was around—most of my fraternity brothers took time off from their busy social lives and actually went to class—I'd listen to comedy albums on the stereo in our room. I loved Bill Cosby's first album with his amazing Noah routine, and I devoured Bob Newhart's *Button-Down Mind* albums. But the first comedy album I ever bought, the one I wore out, listened to it probably five thousand times, was Steve Martin's *Let's Get Small*.

Looking back, I realize that listening to these albums over and over was my college education.

I'd created my own course in comedy, and these albums were my text-books. I studied these great comedians in depth. I heard things in all of them that went beyond their brilliant jokes.

I picked up how to tell a story from Cosby and how to wait for a laugh. I learned more about timing and how to slow way down from Newhart. From Steve Martin I learned the most valuable lesson of all: In order to succeed in comedy, you have to be fearless.

As I listened to these comics over and over, and heard the howls of laughter and roaring applause that showered them, I knew that this was my calling. I needed to get up in front of an audience and per-form. I'd always been able to make people laugh. All I had to do now was take the next step. Arrange a time and place, get up in front of a few friends, and go for it.

Easy enough.

One problem. I panicked.

My calling started to call a little softer.

Maybe it wasn't my calling after all. In fact, I heard something else calling me. A louder call. I was going to go after *that*. My real love, my real calling. It was what I was meant to be all along.

A singer.

A singer like Barry Manilow.

No question I had the voice, the style, the presence to be a singer. I hired an accompanist, a real professional, paid him in beer. Worked up a song sheet. Put the word out at the frat house: Bill Engvall in Concert, Friday night, 9.00 P.M.

Didn't need a stage. I'd just come out on the front porch of the fra-ternity house and sing. The word spread. By nine o'clock, fifty of my fraternity brothers, curiosity seekers, and sadists who love a good train wreck gathered on the lawn. I had a Mr. Microphone set up next to my accompanist, who sat at a portable keyboard. He tinkled a few preliminary chords, my cue. I came out on the porch to thunderous and possibly drunken applause. I bowed slightly, grabbed the mike, and began singing "Mandy." More applause. I bowed again. The crowd loved me. See, I knew it. This was my calling.

I closed my eyes and bent my whole body into the song: *"Ohhh Mandy . . . "*

Yeah. They were digging this.

Wait.

Was that . . . laughter? Were people *laughing?*

No way. Couldn't be. Because I was good. I was better than good. I was great.

"Ohhhhhhhh Mandyyyyyyyy . . ."

That *was* laughter. Hold on. Did they think I was doing a comedy act?

Naw. They were laughing because I was so good. Yeah, that was it.

I finished the last part of "Mandy," took a bow, and began belting "Copacabana." Now they were laughing *and* singing along. Totally into it.

No question about it. They were feeling me.

I must have been delusional, drunk, tone deaf, or all three, because I decided to pursue my singing career.

Seemed logical. I'd memorized all of Barry Manilow's greatest hits, and I had an accompanist who'd work for a six-pack. Plus, I'd caught a break. Someone told me that there was an opening for a singer at a club in Austin. I decided to audition.

The club was in downtown Austin, a hiccup from the statehouse, and only a short ride from campus. One rainy afternoon, I stuffed my sheet music into the glove compartment of my Falcon and drove to the club. I walked in, took my place with a couple of other wannabe singers, and waited to be called. The other two were pacing and thrumming their throats, warming up with a whole slew of vocal exercises. The only vocal exercise I ever did was talk.

"How y'all doin'?"

One waved and walked away; the other pointed to her throat, shook her head, and started trilling a hideous rendition of "Do-Re-Mi." That was my cue to escape to the parking lot and light up a cig. In mid-drag, a waiter at the club summoned me into the club. I was up.

I walked into the main room, which was about the size of a grain elevator, nodded at the owner, who was sitting at a ringside table, and started singing my surefire opening number, "I Write the Songs."

I was *on*. I could feel it. I was nailing that sucker. I peeked at the owner to size him up a little better. He was a round, balding man with a kind face and a genuine smile. I couldn't tell for sure, but he seemed to be into my singing. I thought I even caught him tapping his foot. I was pumped up. He must've liked what he heard, because he let me finish the entire song. He didn't interrupt, take a phone call, or talk to anyone else. I ended the song and said, "Thank you. Thank you very much."

He smiled and said in a gentle, almost soothing voice, "You know what? We already got one Barry Manilow."

I felt as if I'd been kicked in the stomach.

"Oh," I said.

"But I'll say this, you got guts."

I was crushed. Because I knew what he meant. He was giving me his professional opinion based on years of experience:

I sucked.

My singing career made me realize one true thing: What turned me on was the audience response. I knew that I wanted to be an entertainer.

I decided to go for broke. I got permission to perform one night in a small room in the basement of the Student Union. This time I'd eliminate any singing and just go for laughs. I worked up a fifteen-minute

set of some of the worst jokes ever written. I wasn't going for bad jokes intentionally. They just came out that way. Some of the gems:

I put a trash bag over my head and said I was Jim Jones coming home for Christmas. Sick. I pulled off the trash bag and tied on an Indian headband and said I was Chief Big Thing and told an old Indian joke, the one with the famous punch line, "Ass too high, deer run too fast."

The jokes went downhill from there. I don't want to exaggerate, but I'd say this was the worst fifteen minutes of comedy ever performed in the history of the universe.

The crowd loved it.

Each time I opened my mouth and another string of unfiltered garbage came spewing out, the audience went nuts. Granted, this was a friendly crowd made up of friends and fraternity brothers, most of whom were inebriated. I didn't care, and it didn't matter that my material was weak, my delivery mediocre, my timing clunky. What mattered was the laughs. This time I knew that singing Barry Manilow songs was a detour, something that from this moment on I'd have to restrict to the privacy of my shower.

The moment I stood in front of the crowd at the Southwestern Student Union, blurting out bad jokes, I saw a vision of my future. I saw myself standing in front of other crowds of people I actually didn't know, strangers like the ones in the tour groups I messed with in Inner Space Caverns, people who would just laugh because I was funny. I didn't know when, didn't know where, but I *knew*.

Someday it was destined to happen.

29. RIP CORD

In college, I made Dean's list.

Dean was a guy in our frat house who each semester rated the Top Ten party animals in the fraternity. First semester I made Dean's list at number seven. Second semester I climbed to number four with a bullet. If I'd stayed in college all four years, I know I would've had a lock on number one.

Rick made Dean's list, too. Actually, Rick was special. We called him the Bicentennial Man because he managed to achieve a grade point average of .76. Rick could also chug two longnecks at the same time, which made him close to a legend. I mean, how many people are famous for *two* things?

Kinda made me jealous because I'm actually very competitive. I always strive to be the best, no matter what I'm doing. If I'm throwing a party, I want it to be the party of the year. If I'm doing standup, I want the audience to walk away thinking they've just seen the best show ever. I even wanted to be the best nightclub singer. I wanted to be a better Barry Manilow than Barry Manilow. That nightclub owner was right. There was room for only one Barry Manilow. I wanted it to be me.

I was biding my time in college, I knew that. I knew that I wasn't ever going to complete my education. I started to realize that I was on a search. What I was looking for was myself. I wasn't sure where to look, but I was convinced I wasn't going to find me in college.

By this time, my only connection to college was that I lived in the fraternity house. I ate dinner there, which was served about an hour after I woke up. I still served as social chairman with Rick and took all my calls and got my mail there. My frat house was my family. But I knew, unlike with my real family, it was only a matter of time before I would be shown the door. Unless I decided to leave before I got tossed, which is ultimately what I did.

But it ain't over until the fat lady tallies up your grade point average. I still had three months left to party. There were at least a dozen girls on campus that I hadn't dated yet. I had to get busy.

As we've discussed, every guy has three basic needs: eating, sleeping, and sex. And when it comes to sex, a guy will do anything just for the remote *possibility* of sex. At least I would. If I saw a glimmer of hope, if there was a 1 percent chance of sex, I'd go for it.

For weeks, I had my eye on a girl named Lianne. Lianne was brunette, bubbly, and wild. I kept asking her to go out with me and she kept turning me down. All the more reason to keep asking her.

"You never give up, do you?" she said.

"We're meant for each other," I said. "Why fight it?"

Lianne laughed. "Tell you what. I'm going parachuting Saturday afternoon. Why don't you come with me?"

"Parachuting? Out of a plane?"

"No," she said. "Out of a Winnebago. Of course out of a plane."

"Have you done this before?"

"Couple times. And I'm still alive."

"As tempting as it sounds, I'm gonna pass."

"It's totally safe. And it's amazing. There you are, floating down to earth through the clouds, everything out of your control. It's such a rush. I get so *horny.*"

"What time you want me to pick you up?"

At around two in the afternoon, Lianne and I arrived at a shack located at the edge of an open parched field. A sign in one of the windows in faded stenciled letters read: HANK'S PARACHUTING SCHOOL.

"This is it?" I was starting to have second, third, and fourth thoughts. Then I remembered why I was here: If I jumped out of a plane with Lianne, there might be a *chance* of her going out with me.

"So what's the deal? I drink a few beers, strap on a chute, and jump?"

"Somethin' like that, yeah." Lianne laughed. She narrowed her eyes and threw her head back just a little. She had this deep, sexy voice and a contagious laugh. Risking my life was so worth a shot with her.

Of course, even Hank's Parachuting School wouldn't let you jump out of a plane without proper precaution and training. Hank himself gave me his complete parachute jumping course, which took nearly an hour. Hank was tall and thin with pasty skin. He looked like Keith Richards. He wore a torn leather flight jacket and chain-smoked. During the lesson, he actually encouraged me to drink.

"I think you'll enjoy your first jump more if you're pretty hammered," he said.

"Roger," I said, snapping open a longneck.

"You probably don't remember much of the lesson, anyway."

I downed my beer, opened another. "Not a word," I said.

In an hour, we were in a prop job, circling the open patch of brown land, our target. In the shell of the plane, Hank had arranged all the jumpers by weight. Lianne, the lightest, would jump first. I, the heaviest, would go last.

"Isn't this great?" Lianne shouted above the roar of the propellers.

"So great. Amazingly great. Why even jump, this is so great?"

Lianne threw back her head and laughed her deep, sexy, throaty laugh. Suddenly Hank appeared and yelled, "Go!"

Lianne gave me the thumbs-up and leaped out of the plane. She plummeted toward earth, corkscrewed her body in midair, flipped, twisted . . . and then her chute opened. Damn. It was like she was in the flying circus.

Then, one by one, the other jumpers came to the edge of the wing and jumped. Finally, it was my turn.

My stomach flipped. My knees began to shake. I started to sweat as if I were in a steam bath.

"You know what, Hank? I'm suddenly sober. And I got an idea."

"What?"

"Let's go home."

"You can do it, Sundance," Hank said.

"I don't think so. I'm not in the mood to plunge to my death."

"What's Lianne gonna think if you chicken out? You want a chance with her or not?"

"How'd you know that's why I'm doing this?"

Hank stared at me as if I were an idiot. "I'm a *guy*," he said, and shoved me out of the plane.

"AHHHHHHHHH!" I screamed.

Then my mind went blank.

I looked down and I could see the pattern of the earth. It was like being two thousand feet above a giant globe.

My body accelerated. I was rocketing now, falling toward the ground at warp speed. I opened my mouth to scream again. Nothing came out. Those ads for the movie *Alien* were right. In space, no one can hear you scream. Including you.

What the hell am I doing? I thought. *This is nuts. This was not worth it. No girl is worth it. But she sure is cute. So what? She ain't goin' out with me if I'm buried nine feet in the dirt. What was I thinking? I am such a dumb-ass—*

Suddenly, I was yanked backward. My chute burst open, and then I was floating as if I were in a dream and my heart left my mouth and returned to my chest, where after a few minutes it stopped pounding like the bass line of a hip-hop song. I hit the ground, went into a perfect roll, got right to my feet, and gathered up my chute, all in one motion.

I looked to my left and saw Lianne, standing in the middle of the field, holding her chute against her cute thigh. She smiled invitingly, and then she started to applaud.

"Bill Engvall, you rule," she said. "You are the *man.*"

I smiled back and, doing my best John Wayne impression, wiped my mouth and sauntered over to her. "How about we have a couple drinks to celebrate, maybe get some dinner?"

"I can't," Lianne said. "I'm going out with Rick tonight. You know him, he's probably still sleeping. You want to jump again?"

My knees buckled, and then I felt a headache coming on like a freight train roaring through a tunnel. Despite the searing pain in my brain, I somehow got to my car. I opened the trunk, pulled out my cooler, and drank a six-pack of Lone Stars, one after another. About five beers in, I got reflective.

Well, I thought, *I gave it a shot. I lost—but I lived. Would I ever do something this stupid again for a girl?*

I popped open the last beer and said aloud, "Hell yes."

30. ROLLER DERBY QUEEN

I loved watching *Roller Derby* on TV. It was such a great sport. I couldn't tell you one rule. I swear they made it up as they went along. I knew that one of the key positions was "jammer" and that the Roller Derby queens were far more vicious than the guys. I also knew that every game miraculously ended up 35–34, with one of the teams always pulling out a victory at the very end. It was uncanny. I would sit in the living room of our frat house, glued to *Roller Derby*. For some reason, I enjoyed watching women in tight pants and helmets smacking each other real hard. Call me quirky.

I must've been inspired by the Roller Derby, because at one of our frat parties I had a sudden urge to strap on my skates, roller-skate through the house, and try to get physical. Maybe I'd find a girl who'd want to play Roller Derby with me. That was my goal, anyway.

I laced up my skates, polished off my beer, and began skating circles in the living room. I noticed Rick standing by the couch, holding court with three hotties. Easy target. I got into a crouch, Roller Derby style, crunched myself into a human torpedo, pushed off, and bee-lined for the redhead on Rick's right.

Out of the corner of his eye, he saw me coming and yanked the girls out of my path. I swerved to avoid hitting an innocent bystander and skidded to a stop right next to the couch.

That's when I saw her.

The vision of my future.

She was blond and beyond beautiful. Hell, she left beautiful in the dust. She was *riveting*. It was as if everyone else at the party suddenly froze in the middle of what they were doing and faded away and she was the only person in the room.

She sat on the couch, sipping a beer, her leg in a cast. Our eyes met for just a moment. Caught, she lowered her glance and turned away. After a second, she turned back and sort of peeked at me. She was giving me an opening.

I had to say something. Something . . . not lame. I felt my hands sweat slightly. For some reason, it was really important that I didn't sound like a jerk to this girl. Then, maybe it was the beer, but suddenly I felt confident, even cocky. No way I was gonna blow this. No way.

"Hey," I said.

"Hey," she said.

"I'm Bill."

"Gail."

I smiled my killer irresistible smile, the one that showed almost no teeth. "So." I paused. "You wanna go skating?"

Gail raised an eyebrow. "No."

"No?"

"No." She nodded at her leg. "My foot's in a cast."

I scratched my head and nodded at her cast. "I didn't mean *now*. I meant . . . sometime."

"Not really," Gail said, smiling back. What a smile. Mannnn . . .

"Anyway." Gail had turned away and was resuming a conversation I'd apparently interrupted. I stood at the foot of the couch, shot down and speechless.

"So no skating, then," I said. I felt like a punch-drunk fighter throwing a last desperate left hook, hoping for a miraculous knockout.

Gail turned and gave me a different kind of smile. This one was less warm, less kind. This one gave me a wordless but clear message:

"You're a dumb-ass."

it doesn't take much to infect you. That's what happened to me. I could've stayed at college, kept partying, and put off the inevitable, but I was too driven, too intent on trying to make a go of it.

First thing, though, I had to break the news to Dad. I was dreading this conversation. I'm not sure what he had in mind for me as a career, but I doubted standup comedian was on his short list. And when I told him I was leaving school, his alma mater, I was pretty sure he wasn't going to throw me a parade.

I dropped the bomb one night at dinner. His reaction shocked me.

"Well, maybe it's for the best."

"What? Did you hear what I said? I'm quitting school."

"I heard you. Believe me, I'm not thrilled, but if this is what you want to do, now's the time. You're young. Go for it."

"Really?"

"Yep. If you don't, you'll always regret it."

Just when I thought I had Dad figured out, he'd do or say something that'd ambush me. Usually in a good way.

"Thanks, Dad," I said. "Oh, that forty grand a year you were spending to send me to college? You wouldn't want to keep giving it to me, would you? Since you planned on spending it anyway—"

Dad stared at me the way a snake looks at a field mouse.

"I'm kidding, Dad. That was a joke. But I will write better jokes, I swear."

"You'll have to," he said.

So with his blessing, I left college and moved to Dallas.

I found a small apartment, a studio, which sounds cool but is really just a fancy word meaning your bedroom, living room, dining room, and kitchen are crammed together into a fifty-square-foot cubicle. It also means that your bed, couch, and kitchen table are the same thing. It didn't matter, though, because I wasn't home much. I'd hit pay dirt on my first try. I found a job on the outskirts of show business.

I sold radio time. On commission. I worked in a boiler room elbow

31. EMIL FROM THE KITCHEN

All good things come to an end. Including the two-year nonstop party I like to call college. It was time to move on. I decided that I was going to leave Southwestern at the beginning of the summer and move to Dallas.

The fact is, I'd gotten bitten by the show business bug. It had hit me big time. I could trace the first sting all the way back to third grade and my starring role in "Clementine," then to Bobbie Brown's creative writing class in high school, and finally up to my feeble attempts at singing and standup in college. I know this: Once you're bitten, to elbow with eleven sweaty people, all screaming at the top of their lungs into telephones. We read from a script. During training, our boss drilled us into believing that if we didn't stick to the script, we'd be taken outside behind the building and shot. I must have believed him, because I didn't dare ad-lib. I read from the script, word for word. Well, nearly.

"Hello, Mr. Buford, this is Bill Engvall over at WCRP. How you do-ing? Ouch, that sounds nasty. I'll bet some K-Y jelly will clear that right up. Hey, before you know it, it'll be that time again when all the kids will be going back to school. Blink once and the little buggers will be off to college. Anyway, we're going to be putting a message out over the air to remind people to drive safely, and it could be sponsored by you! How about that? Mr. Buford, can I count on you to be one of our sponsors?"

Mr. Buford would then say, "Huh. That sounds okay. Can I adver-tise something? Because I'd like to mention my bait shop. Every Wednesday I have a special. Two worms for the price of one. And don't forget our weekly drawing for a free lure."

"Uh, no. You can't advertise anything. It's a public service an-nouncement."

"Then I ain't doin' it. Screw it."

"Well, okay, then. Have a nice day, Mr. Butt Ford."

I lasted three days.

I made a quick comeback. At the end of the week, I auditioned for my first professional acting gig—and I got hired on the spot. At least I think I auditioned. I know I got hired.

I read an ad on a supermarket bulletin board that said: "Actors wanted for children's theater company. Experience preferred but not required."

This sounded perfect. I tore off the phone number at the bottom of the flyer, called up, and got the address. About two hours later I was sitting in a Motel 6 along with three other actors, Phil and Madeline, the husband and wife who ran the company, and Hobo, their dog, a German shepherd and collie mix who instantly fell in love with my leg. The play they were doing was *Rumpelstiltskin,* which they were going to perform over the next six weeks at a bunch of schools all over the state. The actors would play multiple roles and travel together with the scenery, props, and Hobo in Phil and Madeline's beat-up VW van. The pay would be twenty-five dollars a week.

"Any questions?" Phil asked.

I looked at the other three actors. They looked at me. I shrugged. "No," I said.

"Good," Phil said. "You're all hired."

I left the motel room on Cloud Nine. I assumed that Madeline and Phil were such great judges of talent that they could tell I was a gifted actor just by looking at me. Turned out that they needed me for other reasons. For one, Phil had a bad back, and Madeline and I were the only people in the company strong enough to lift the scenery out of the van and carry it into the schools. Also, Hobo took a liking to me. I've always loved animals, and Hobo and I bonded. I fed him, walked him, and got him to stay, a good thing, because I was the only one who could keep him from biting the children.

The play was a hoot and a major step up from selling radio time. I was a *paid* performer, incredible after only one week in show business. I played several parts, one of which was Emil from the kitchen. I had the best line in the play. The Queen would ask Rumpelstiltskin, "Is there anything you would like, dear?"

Rumpelstiltskin would answer, "Yes. A meal from the kitchen."

I'd come out and say, "You called?"

I'd either get a huge laugh or nothing. Half the time the kids didn't get the joke.

By week four of the six-week gig, I'd had my fill of driving around Texas in the back of a van with six people and a dog, lugging scenery with Madeline, who never really held up her end, Phil's back ailment that seemed to improve after a few beers, and the screaming, shouting, spitball-throwing audiences of seven-year-olds. My attitude had become *Okay, this was great, but it can end.*

After the tour of *Rumpelstiltskin* finished, Madeline and Phil asked me to re-up for their next production, *Cinderella*, with Madeline playing the title role. Even though Phil offered me the part of the "funny" Fairy Godmother, I turned it down. I really liked Phil and Madeline and all the other actors, but I wanted to branch out, try something different.

A friend of mine named Paul had begun making a few bucks modeling for department store catalogs. His agent had seen my picture and wanted to meet me. At first this sounded great. Then it sounded fishy. Paul had what I'd call a male model look, I can't exactly describe the look, but I know this: I didn't have it. I looked more like one of the guys in the Allman Brothers band. Every time I tried to picture myself posing in some stylish golf duds, a babe on each arm, or wearing a Ralph Lauren polo shirt and a new pair of Hagar slacks at a cocktail party while sipping a drink with an umbrella in it, I couldn't see it. The picture got all blurry. Still, if the agent dude wanted to meet me, why not?

After about ten seconds, I knew the agent didn't envision me as a male model wearing golf clothes. He envisioned me as a male model wearing *no* clothes.

"Take your shirt off," the agent said.

"Uh . . . *what?*"

"If I'm going to be your agent, I have to see what I'm selling."

"Shoot," I said. "I forgot. I'm supposed to have sex with my *girlfriend.* Damn. I'm late. Gotta run."

And run I did. Out of his office, out of the building, to my car, and over to Paul's house, where we had a little chat. Paul was horrified.

"He *what?*"

"You heard me. He wanted me to take my shirt off." I took a swig of my Lone Star.

"Damn," Paul said.

"You know what I think?" I polished off the beer and eased the empty down on his kitchen counter. "I think he might be gay."

"Huh," Paul said, mulling over the possibility. "That would explain it."

"He ain't my type, I'll tell you that."

"I had no idea. Look, I owe you."

"Forget it. These things happen." I opened his fridge and pulled out another beer. "Well, okay, you owe me."

"I'm gonna make up for it. I promise."

Turned out that he did.

32. IT HAPPENED ONE NIGHT

Paul must've felt really guilty, because he made up for it big time.

He got me a part in a movie.

It wasn't a major role or anything. It wasn't even a speaking part. In fact, all you can see are my feet.

The movie was *Logan's Run*, a science fiction thriller starring Michael York, Richard Jordan, Roscoe Lee Browne, Farrah Fawcett, and me. The movie is set in the future where there's a law that everybody over the age of thirty has to be killed. At one point, a bunch of thirty-year-olds make a run for it. I'm one. You see me running. Well, you see my *feet*, and then suddenly I—my feet—break into a cartwheel.

That's it.

I'd like to thank the Academy . . .

My whole part lasts three seconds—we had the premiere at Paul's apartment, and we timed it—but everyone agreed: It was a heckuva cartwheel. So good that it got me a paycheck and an agent, who somehow managed to get me cast in a couple of other movies. Ones in which I spoke.

With only a cartwheel to work with, he must've been a pretty good agent. I was on my way. I wasn't in a huge hurry, though, because a few weeks after leaving college, I found a great job: spinning records in a nightclub. It was the mid-1970s and disco was king. All over Dallas, nightclubs modeling themselves on New York's famous Studio 54 were popping up like mushrooms. It was all about cashing in on the *Saturday Night Fever* craze.

Our nightclub was right in the heart of the trend, and I was right in the heart of our nightclub. I controlled the sounds. I stood at my DJ perch, high above a dance floor edged with blinking lights, the disco ball spinning overhead, strobe lights pulsating like blinding neon lasers. I played all the disco hits from Donna Summer to the Bee Gees to "Disco Duck."

I loved this job because I didn't just play the music, I also messed around, doing snappy patter between the songs. I kept my comments to a minimum because people were there to dance, but I got in my share. People knew the music wasn't canned; there was an actual human playing the records. Every once in a while someone would come up to me and say, "You're funny," and it would make my night. Of course, they were always slurring their words, on the verge of passing out, but that didn't matter.

One of the perks of the job was that my boss let me drink for free. This explained why I would often come by on my nights off and hang out at the bar. One night, I was sitting at the bar with a friend of mine named John. The bartender pulled a couple of draft beers into mugs and slid them over to us.

"Hey, Bill. Did you hear they opened a comedy club down the road? They're packed every night."

"I went last week," John said. "Amateur night. Man, most of those comics *sucked.* Hey, Bill, you ought to go up."

"Why, I'm so bad I qualify?"

"I meant there's no competition for you. Those comics aren't even in your league."

"Nice save." I sipped my beer thoughtfully. "I suppose we could go watch."

After another beer and no action at the bar, we decided to head over to the comedy club. When we got there, we found that the place was sold out and there was a crowd outside clamoring to get in.

"Oh well, it was a nice idea," I said. "Let's go."

"You don't know anything, do you?" John reached out his hand and jiggled his fingers as if he had an itch. "Give me twenty bucks."

"Huh?"

"Watch and learn."

I reached into my pocket, pulled out a twenty, and handed it to John. He walked over to Kevin, a security guard the size of a small building who was blocking the door and most of the moon. John said something to him, pointed at me, then slipped Kevin the twenty. Kevin nodded at me, smiled, and disappeared inside the club. John walked back to me, a cartoon-like grin covering his face.

"We're in."

"Oh really? Last I saw, Kevin took my twenty and went inside looking for the buffet."

"Be cool."

A moment later, a huge mitt of a hand appeared at the door signaling us to come in. A sea of people standing between us and the door of the club miraculously parted. Kevin stepped out and escorted us into the club to our table, which was ringside, practically on the stage.

"Thanks, man," John said.

"The pleasure is mine," Kevin said. He smiled at me again. I smiled back, and Kevin ducked his head and blushed. "Could I have your autograph?"

"I told him who you were," John said.

I looked at him blankly.

"Star of *Logan's Run*," John said. "He's so modest."

"I'm a big movie fan," Kevin said. "What was it like working with Farrah Fawcett?"

"She's great. We dated for a while, but then the movie wrapped and I had to move on. She was devastated. She's still stalking me."

I thought Kevin was about to pass out.

"Here," I said and scribbled my name on a cocktail napkin.

Kevin blushed again. He extended his paw. I shook it. "First round's on me," he mumbled, and hustled back to his post outside the theater.

The lights dimmed, and the emcee came out and introduced the first of a string of comics, each one about as funny as a disease. At one point, Sonny, the owner of the nightclub where I worked, came by and sat at our table. Sonny was a heavy man with a mole on his forehead the size of a baseball. Sonny was always in a good mood.

"How'd you guys score such a good table?"

"The doorman confused Engvall with a movie star."

"Robert Redford," I said.

"See, that's what I'm talking about. That right there is funnier than anything these monkeys could come up with. Why don't you go up?"

"Nah. It's my night off."

"Come *on*. You're funny. Show 'em what you got."

"I'm just here to watch."

Sonny looked at me. "You know what your problem is? You're not drunk enough. Where's the waitress?" He caught her eye. "Ma'am, excuse me! Could we get two more beers? Thanks. You want a beer, John?"

I said, "I'm telling you, Sonny, I'm just gonna watch."

Sonny stood up and swatted me on the bank. Then he winked at John. "Sure, Bill. Suit yourself."

Sonny must've known something, because two beers later, I turned to John and said simply, "You're right. I'm as good as they are."

I shot out of my chair and found Joyce, a petite redhead who ran the club. I told her I wanted a slot. She grunted, barely looked at me, and penciled my name onto her clipboard. "You're up at ten-oh-five," she said. "Wait by the bar."

"Okay. Thanks. What do I do?"

"Be funny," she said.

I forced a smile and made my way to the bar. I ordered a beer but didn't drink it. I stood at the bar, my back to the stage, toying with my drink, looking inside the glass for inspiration, trying to figure out what I would say. I thought of a few jokes, abandoned them because I remembered I'd heard them in the third grade. I started to laugh because I couldn't think of anything to say. Not a thing. My mind was a total blank.

Great, I thought. *I'll just get up there and stare at the audience for five minutes. I'd still be funnier than anyone else tonight.*

I turned back, saw that our table was empty, then searched the room for John. I found him in the corner, coming on to the waitress. I shook my head. John had a way with the ladies. I smiled. At least one of us would get lucky tonight.

Then I heard Joyce announce my name. I pushed myself away from the bar like it was the side of a swimming pool and jogged toward the stage, a smattering of applause at my back. For a moment, I thought of cartwheeling onto the stage, but thought better of it and simply leaped up. Bad move. I misjudged my jump and nearly missed the stage. I grabbed onto the microphone stand for support and steadied myself, and, as I did, I vaguely heard the sound of laughter. Okay, they were laughing *at* me, but they were laughing. It was a start.

I began to speak. I heard myself tell one of the jokes that went over well when I performed at the Student Union. Another laugh.

And then time stopped.

What happened next can only be described as an out-of-body experience. My mind started to float up and hover above my body. It was weird. I saw this guy, Bill Engvall, doing standup on stage, at this comedy club, but it was as if I were watching myself from the audience. I was there . . . but not there.

I saw my mouth moving, and I heard jokes flowing out with ease and confidence because the crowd was laughing. Really laughing. I saw me pacing the stage, shaking my head, telling an old joke, one I knew always got a laugh, then getting bold and ad-libbing something about an old girlfriend, then doing an impression of one of my buddies, and still the audience laughed. As I watched me from my seat in the audience, I almost said aloud, "Hey, that guy's doing well. That guy's funny! That guy's *me!*"

My five minutes ended. I bowed and grinned, and the audience applauded, and I started to leave the stage, and Joyce said to the crowd, "Bill Engvall, ladies and gentlemen, BILL ENGVALL!" I bowed again, and the audience applauded louder. I made my way back to the bar, walking on air, and ordered a shot of whiskey.

"Hey, man, you were funny," the bartender said.

"Thank you," I said. "I have no idea what I said. That's the truth. I don't remember a thing."

I don't know why I confessed that to the bartender. Sometimes the easiest and safest people to talk to are strangers. I drained the whiskey in one swallow, and Joyce, John, and Sonny, my new fan club, all appeared.

"You were great," John roared, pounding me on the back as if he were giving me the Heimlich maneuver.

"I had a feeling," Sonny said, grabbing my hand and shaking it. He smiled at Joyce. "I knew he was funny. I knew it."

Joyce was beaming. "So, funny boy," she said. "How'd you like to be my regular emcee?"

I stared at her. "It's loud in here. What did you say?"

"I believe she just offered you a job," Sonny said.

"House emcee," Joyce said.

"What do I have to do?"

"You pick up the comics that I book for the week at the airport, drive them here, emcee the show, and drive them back to the airport at the end of the week. I'll pay you two seventy-five a week."

I looked at Sonny. He answered for me. "This is what you want, isn't it? Besides, I can't afford to pay you that much."

"You sure? I don't want to leave you in the lurch."

"Don't worry. I'll find some other schmuck to spin records."

It took me a full two seconds to think over Joyce's offer. It sounded too good to be true: I'd work at night, I could drink on the job, sleep late, and I'd get to perform comedy. It was my dream job.

"When do I start?"

"Is tomorrow too soon?"

"That'll work."

"Here. Sign my contract." Joyce reached out her hand. I shook it. Joyce grinned and slipped away into the crowd. Sonny headed off to the men's room; John went off to close the deal with the waitress. I pointed at the bartender for another shot. I sighed. This night was unreal. I'd just gotten hired as an emcee at a comedy club. It was great. Beyond great. It was mind-blowing. There I was, standing at the bar, celebrating the best night of my life—alone.

"Hey."

I turned at the sound of her voice. I blinked once. I had almost forgotten her. Almost. Beauty that riveting is something that stays with you. The impression she'd made was indelible, like a scar.

"Gail," she said, dipping her head shyly.

"I remember. Bill."

She smiled. "I know. I was in the audience."

"Wow. Who you here with?"

"Friends. We were in the mood for a couple of laughs."

"Why'd you come here?"

She laughed. "Yeah, it was kind of a mistake until you—" She stopped.

"What?"

"Came on. You were *good.*"

"You're just saying that because of how well we hit it off last time. We're so close you don't want to hurt my feelings."

"Exactly."

She was smiling. And she wasn't leaving.

"You can tell me the truth. You can tell me if I sucked. I can take it. I'm very thick-skinned. I'm like a turtle."

"You didn't *suck.* I mean, you're not Robin Williams—"

I grabbed my stomach in mock pain. "*Ow, ow, ow.* That hurt."

"Well, you asked."

"Yeah, but I was lying. Now you've done it. Only one thing you can do now to fix this."

"And that is?"

"Let me buy you a drink."

Gail craned her neck toward the center of the club, where her friends were clustered around a table. A couple of them stood up and started gathering their stuff. "Thanks, but I think we're actually getting ready to go."

I smiled. "Okay."

Gail looked down at the bar and hesitated for a split second. "But I'll take a rain check."

"I'll call you." I grabbed a two-drink-minimum card (which Gail still has) and pulled out a pen.

"You always carry a pen?"

"Oh yeah. For autographs."

"You sign a lot of autographs?"

"So far, one. But you never know. What's your number?" She told it to me. I scribbled it on the card. I wrote mine below it, then tore the card in half. "I wrote mine, too, just in case."

"Good." Gail stood up, and smiled. I glanced quickly at her leg.

"Your cast is gone."

"Yeah. Finally."

"Your leg healed up real nice."

As soon as I said that, I blushed. Then Gail blushed, too, and we both starting smiling and staring at the floor. She looked up and took a breath. "Okay, so." She waved and headed toward her friends.

I yelled after her. "I'll call you soon. Couple of weeks."

33. DEMON LOVER

I called her the next day.

I invited her to join me on the set of my movie.

Well, okay, it wasn't exactly *my* movie.

I had gotten a part in a movie that was shooting in and around Dallas. It was called *Split Image* and starred James Woods, Peter Fonda, Karen Allen, Brian Dennehy, and Michael O'Keefe. The plot involved Michael O'Keefe as an impressionable young man who falls under the spell of a charismatic Jim Jones type played by Peter Fonda, joins a religious cult, and becomes brainwashed. Fun for the whole family.

I was hired as Michael O'Keefe's stand-in because of my incredible acting ability and because we were about the same height. What this meant was that I spent most of my day baking in the Texas summer heat standing on Michael O'Keefe's camera marks while the crew moved around me setting up lights and adjusting camera angles. Suffering potential heatstroke and exposing myself to skin cancer on a daily business? Didn't matter. I was in show business.

Plus, I wasn't just Michael O'Keefe's stand-in. My talents as an actor weren't wasted. I also had a supporting role, crucial to the story.

I played the best college kid in the whole world, maybe ever. I know because in the script my character's name was "College Kid #1."

I had a whole scene with Michael O'Keefe, a very dramatic, emotional scene in which I got to show my acting range. I'm now going to reprint the entire scene for you. Get out your hankies.

In the scene, I'm standing near a bunch of my friends, other college students. Michael O'Keefe approaches me.

MICHAEL O'KEEFE: Hi.

ME: Hi.

MICHAEL O'KEEFE: Can I talk to you about our beliefs?

ME: Sure.

That's it.

Take a minute to compose yourselves.

There are obviously many ways to play this scene, many interpretations. I must've nailed it on the first take, because the director, Ted Kotcheff, said, "That was great. Let's move on." Clearly, I had a knack for this acting thing.

The day I asked Gail to visit me on the set was a special day. I planned it that way. I'm not a fool. My big scene with Michael O'Keefe was in the can, and I knew she probably had better things to do than watch me stand in the hot sun for hours at a time. I asked her to visit me that day because I had been given yet another part in the movie.

I was going to play a slimy, scary monster.

I don't know why, but I thought Gail might enjoy watching that.

Here's the background leading up to my new scene.

Michael O'Keefe's parents abduct him from the cult and bring him to a motel, where he is going to be deprogrammed by James Woods. The scene starts. James Woods begins deprogramming in his unique, intense, scary way. Michael O'Keefe is watching him, staring at him, his eyes are sort of flying back in his head—

Suddenly, James Woods turns into a vile, horrifying demon, complete with claws, red eyes, and a humongous tongue that shoots out.

I played the demon.

I asked Gail to meet me in makeup. I was going to be in there for four hours. I figured we could hang out and talk while I was getting into demon-wear.

She showed up a couple of hours into the process, and I introduced her to Connie, my makeup artist. I think Gail would admit that this was a kind of cool first date. I actually hesitate calling it a date because we were just hanging out in the makeup trailer, talking and laughing as if we'd known each other for years. That's the thing about Gail and me. After that disastrous first meeting, when I was drunk and clueless, we just sort of slid into a relationship. I had never felt so at ease with another person. Ever. It wasn't just me, either. I know Gail felt it, because we've talked about it over the years. And I know Connie thought we were either longtime lovers or the very best of friends, because she asked Gail to help her take my pants off.

"Come on, honey," Connie said. "We need to get the bottom of his costume on. Help me get his pants off."

I silently whispered, *Thank you, Lord*, but outwardly I shrugged and looked at Gail helplessly. "I'd do it myself, but—"

I held up my hands to show her my problem. They were encased in demon claws. Connie saw Gail hesitate, then she shrugged, too.

"Grab a leg," Connie said.

Gail blushed a little. Well, okay, her face turned the color of a lobster, but she grabbed my pant leg at the ankle and pulled.

"Ow!" I screamed. "That's my privates!"

Now both Connie and Gail laughed. Then Connie nodded at Gail, and simultaneously they tugged off my pants, leaving me standing in the center of the trailer in my demon mask, demon claws, demon torso, and Sesame Street boxer shorts.

They both started laughing harder.

"What? You don't like Big Bird?"

"You planned this," Gail said.

"Nooo. I have a whole Sesame Street collection."

The door to the makeup trailer swung open, and Marvin, a gay production assistant, poked his head in.

"Excuse me. Five minutes. Oh my, it's Big Bird. Where are Bert and Ernie? Never mind. None of my business."

We all lost it. At one point, I caught Gail's eye. It was so weird. We'd only just met, but the look we shared at the moment made me feel as if we'd known each other forever.

After we wrapped for the day, Gail and Connie helped me off with my demon costume. This time there were a million people crammed in the trailer, and I couldn't get back into my street clothes and out of there fast enough. Gail waited outside. We'd planned to have brunch at a place I loved called the Cardinal Pub, which was my favorite spot to eat and drink in Dallas. It was actually a small beer garden, cozy and intimate. Best of all, I could get my favorite drink, a Texas martini, which was a draft beer with an olive in it. Not only did I love the drink itself, I loved the concept. You'd finish your beer, and there was a little prize left in the glass: food. A delicious olive. I don't know who thought of this drink, but it's brilliant. A beer and a treat. Genius.

I pointed this out to Gail as we stayed for about three more hours at the Cardinal Pub. Thing is, we had no idea that three hours had passed. To us it felt like three minutes. We talked, and laughed, and flirted, and talked some more. At some point, an hour in, or two, it didn't really matter, I knew. I just knew.

I knew we were falling in love.

At least I was.

34. BUDDY, BUDDY

After that first three-hour brunch at the Cardinal Pub, Gail and I became inseparable. We'd hang out every day; I'd call her when I got home and get all excited if she showed up at the club. When people asked me if we were going out, I hesitated. We were—I think—but "going out" didn't come close to accurately describing our relationship. We were best friends. We told each other everything. I told her stuff I'd never told anyone. We just fit. So I guess we were the closest of friends and a romantic couple.

Except we didn't actually *do* anything romantically for months.

Oh, I wanted to, believe me, and I would have if she'd have taken off the STOP sign. I was willing to go at her pace, slow and cautious as it was. Hell, she made a snail look like a cheetah. But I cherished our friendship so much and I was so worried about messing things up that I held back. All Gail had to say was, "I'm so afraid of ruining our friendship," and I'd back off faster than if she'd said, "I'm actually a guy."

Then one night I felt the wind shift. It was the night of the *Split Image* wrap party, and of course I invited Gail as my date. The producers went all out. They had a live band, a buffet, and an open bar. Gail and I mingled with the actors, stuffed ourselves at the buffet, and spent a good portion of the evening at the bar. It wasn't our fault. They were serving one of our favorites: watermelon shooters. Love those things. They taste so good, and they sneak up on you. One minute you're enjoying this refreshing teeny little watermelony drink, the next you're flat on your face. They're so great.

That night we found ourselves losing our grip fairly quickly. Before we knew it we were tipsy and silly. We moved away from the bar and headed to the dance floor. We started dancing, and I did my robotic white man's dance where I clench my bottom lip real hard and stick it out in a kind of underbite. I also tried my hand at a couple of John Travolta *Saturday Night Fever* moves. That wasn't pretty, either.

Thankfully, the band cranked the music down and moved into a slow one. Gail and I wrapped our arms around each other and held tight. In my case, I was holding on so I wouldn't fall over.

"You're my best friend," I said.

Gail closed her eyes. "You're mine, too."

"It's fun slow dancing with your best friend," I said. "Big fun. 'Cause you know nothin's gonna happen."

"Don't be so sure about that," Gail said.

Click.

Did I just hear what I thought I heard? I'm sure I did. I may have a bad case of ADD, but I am not hard of hearing.

"You wanna go home?" I whispered.

Gail smiled and, her eyes still closed, said, "Yeah. I do."

I didn't need a map to see where this was going. Tonight was the night.

Me and my best friend were gonna get happy.

We said our good-byes; I thanked the director and hugged Connie the makeup lady, who kissed me and Gail, and Gail and I made our way to the car. We didn't say a word as I opened the door for her, but I was smiling, and when she saw me smiling, she smiled back. We were grinning at each other like a couple of game show hosts. We got into the car, and Gail scooted over, squeezing in against me tight. She grabbed onto my arm, kissed me on the cheek, and leaned her head on my shoulder.

I fumbled with the keys, dropped them on the floor, and kicked them under the seat.

"You okay?"

"I'm fine. Little nervous, maybe. I shouldn't be. I mean, I've done this before."

"I know. I've seen you do it."

I was horrified. "You have?"

"Yeah. Like a thousand times."

I laughed because now I was *very* nervous—and a little creeped out. "Well, a thousand might be high—"

"Well, sure, not literally, but I've seen you start up a car a *lot.*"

I paused. "Oh yeah, that. A thousand might even be right."

I started the car, and we headed down the road toward the freeway. I needed to recharge the romantic mood. I flicked on the radio, twirled the tuner, bumped into ten seconds of static, and then found what I was looking for: Barry Manilow singing "I Write the Songs." Perfect. Back on track.

"I love this song," Gail said.

"I know. *Buddy.*"

I could feel Gail smile as she snuggled against me. I lifted my arm over her head and reached it across her shoulders. Softly, we sang along with Barry, never looking at each other.

We approached the freeway, and I drove up the on-ramp. Her exit was first, a quarter of a mile ahead, then mine, a mile after that. I didn't want to gun the engine to reveal how anxious I was, so I kept the speed steady, but all I could think about was getting to my apartment, parking the car, leading her in, kissing her—

"Where are you going?"

"Huh?"

"We just passed my exit."

"Well . . . yeah. I thought we'd go back to my place and—"

"Uh, *no.* I need to get up early tomorrow."

"Oh."

Gail peered at me. A look of realization came over her face. She pecked me on the check. "Rain check?"

"Seems like we got a lotta rainouts to make up."

"Every game gets played, though, doesn't it?"

"Every one," I said. "And I hope we're not talking about baseball."

Gail yawned and got comfortable. I sighed, headed off the freeway, and started to double back so I could take my buddy home.

It was all right. No way I was going to wreck our friendship. Romance could wait. We'd get there when the time was right.

"I write the songs that make the whole world singggg . . ."

"Shut up, Manilow," I muttered.

I punched OFF on the radio.

35. POPPING THE QUESTION

Dallas was treating me well. I loved my job at the comedy club. I got to sleep in, drink for free, work on my standup, and hang out with some of the best comedians in the world, people like Robin Williams, Jay Leno, and Garry Shandling. I was learning my craft by watching them, by talking comedy with them, and through trial and error onstage. The process was slow but sure; I felt myself improving each week, building my confidence, and finding my voice.

Meanwhile, Gail and I had taken the next step. We'd finally become lovers. She kept her promise.

We did make up one of those rainouts. Amazingly, our friendship not only didn't suffer, it intensified. We actually became better friends. Never thought that'd be possible.

There was something else. I couldn't tell her this, but I had fallen totally ga-ga in love with her. Guys can never admit this. Never say you're all ga-ga and mushy. For some reason, it's a turnoff. Guys need to maintain that macho, tough guy, I-couldn't-care-less exterior. I tried that. Lasted about five seconds. Gail saw through me as if I were made out of Saran Wrap. I just gave in to it. I mean, I knew she was the "one." It was just a matter of time before I'd pop the question.

Finally, one day over Texas martinis at "our place," the Cardinal Pub, I got up the courage.

I didn't come right out with it. I had to run up to it a little. I sort of stared off into space for a while, then stared into my drink and started fooling with my olive.

"What are you doing?" Gail asked me.

"Huh?"

"You've been playing with that olive for about an hour. Either eat it or give it to me."

"I need to ask you something. It's kind of important." I took a deep breath. I took both of her hands in mine. "Gail?"

"Yes, Bill?"

"Do you think you can handle show business?"

"Do I think I can *what*?"

"I really need a woman who can handle show business. It's a brutal business. Takes a certain makeup. You need rhinoceros skin."

She looked at me as if I were speaking Portuguese.

I think I can explain her reaction.

To this point, my show business career consisted of emceeing at a comedy club, where my duties included getting coffee and running errands for the comedians and driving them to and from the airport, parts in three movies totaling three sentences and a cartwheel, and playing Emil from the kitchen in a traveling children's theater company production of *Rumpelstiltskin*.

And I was worried about Gail being able to handle show business? What exactly was I thinking?

She looked at me, squeezed my hands, and said, "Honey, you can count on me."

"I knew I could. Man, I feel so much better. Thanks. You want my olive?"

Two weeks later I asked her another question. This one kind of slipped out and took us both by surprise.

It was my day off, and I picked her up late in the afternoon at her apartment complex. We walked outside, she locked her door, we took two steps, and I dropped down on one knee.

"Gail—"

"Bill, what are you doing? Get up."

"—will you marry me?"

"Are you nuts? *No*."

I paused. "Not the answer I was hoping for, but awright."

"You're serious?"

"I thought I was."

"Oh, Bill . . ."

She looked at me as if I were a pathetic lost puppy. "I love you."

"You do?"

"You know I do."

"I do?"

"Yes," Gail said.

"You realize we both said *I do*? It's almost like we just got married, so we might as well go all the way with it. Make it official. What the hell?"

"You are so romantic. But I think we should wait. We're not ready yet."

"We're not?"

"No, Bill. We will be. Not just yet."

I knew she was right. She made a lot of sense. That was the thing about Gail. She was very sensible. Unlike me. I was nonsensical. In fact, we were total opposites in pretty much everything. A perfect match.

"So no marriage then?"

"Not right now."

"Okay." I paused. *Well, now what?*

I was feeling kind of stuck. After you've proposed to the love of your life and she's turned you down, where do you go from there? I took a shot.

"How about a movie?"

"That works."

"I am so relieved. I'm feeling just a teeny bit vulnerable right now. I didn't want to get my heart broken again."

"Shut up."

"Okay, I will. But I have to ask you one more thing, and this is really important."

"What?"

"Would you help me up? I've lost all feeling in my knee."

36. THE JELLYFISH STUNG ME ON MY PEE-PEE

I believe every serious relationship is like a cross-country flight. You're all excited and nervous during takeoff, then you level off and settle in at a certain cruising altitude where everything seems fine, then without warning you hit a rough patch. Turbulence. The point where you talk about seeing other people and flirting with the flight attendant.

Our relationship was no exception. We reached our tipping point a couple of weeks after I asked Gail to marry me.

When you have the "seeing other people" conversation, there are only two possible results. One, you'll break up within a month because you really do want to see other people because you're sick of each other. The little things she does that you thought were so cute three months ago have become fingernails on a blackboard. The small annoyances that at first made him unique and quirky now make him a lump and a slob. The thrill is gone. The magic has up and left. The monkey would rather stay at home than go outside and play. You get the idea.

Two, you talk about seeing other people because that's what you think you're supposed to do. You never really will see other people. You're just going through the motions.

Which is what happened with Gail and me.

We each tried to date someone else. Some guy asked Gail out, and I met some woman at the club. We went out on our dates the same night, the same time. We spent a grand total of forty minutes with these other people and ended up spending the rest of the night with each other. I made up some ridiculous excuse. I told my date that I had to get home because I had an audition for a play at midnight. To give you some idea of her intelligence, she bought it.

So, after agreeing to see other people, Gail and I started seeing *more* of each other. In fact, we moved in together. This thrilled her parents no end. I think her mom summed it up best:

"You're living in sin with that comedian?"

With the emphasis on "comedian." I think if Gail had said, "Mom, I'm moving in with Bill, the heart surgeon who's independently wealthy," she might not have flipped out so much. I'm just guessing. I know if my daughter told me she was moving in with a comedian, I wouldn't exactly throw her a party.

Once we moved in, we both knew that getting married wasn't that far off. I wasn't sure how far off. I was leaving that up to Gail. I just knew that I wasn't getting down on one knee again. Call me gun shy.

The actual marriage proposal took on a slightly different complexion this time. I was still emceeing at the comedy club, but I'd started playing a few dates at other clubs. I was beginning to spend a fair amount of time out on the road. One afternoon, Gail drove me to the airport to see me off. I was playing a couple of dates in a club in Kansas City. In those days, before September 11, you could wait by the gate until your plane took off. We sat together holding hands, watching planes take off and land.

"My mom is still having a hard time with us living together," Gail said.

"I'm not moving out," I said. "She'd have to physically remove me. I know she's a strong woman, but I think I'd give her a fight."

"Bill Engvall, that is borderline romantic."

"Romantic nothin'. We can't afford two rents. Hey, here's a funny idea. Let's get married. Then we wouldn't be living in sin."

I started laughing because I meant it as a joke. Gail clicked open her purse and pulled out her datebook.

"Next week is tough," she said. "I have two exams. The following week I have to go to that conference. We should probably give people a couple of weeks notice, plus we have to plan stuff. How about the middle of next month? That's six weeks. That should be enough time."

A disconnected metallic voice crackled through a speaker above our heads. "Flight two oh four to Kansas City is now boarding."

"That's my flight," I said.

"Yeah. You gotta go. So does that weekend work for you?"

"Sure," I said. I gathered up my stuff and stood up.

"Good," Gail said. "I'll start getting everything together. I'll call the caterer when I get home."

"Right. Okay. Good."

"Have a good flight. I love you."

"I love you, too."

We kissed good-bye. In a daze, I wandered over to the bored flight attendant who was standing at the door to the plane, taking tickets.

"I think I just got engaged," I said to her.

"Great. Congratulations." She tore off my ticket stub and handed it back to me. I stood frozen in my spot. "You're holding up the line," she said.

"Huh? Oh. Sorry."

I staggered down the hatchway to the plane feeling stunned and giddy all at the same time.

The wedding was a small, intimate, classy affair perfectly put together by Gail. The highlight for me, after kissing Gail, of course, was watching my in-laws' reaction when the limo pulled up to take us to the hotel. I knew a guy who knew a guy who ran a limousine service. This was 1982, before SUV stretch limos the length of a city block existed. The absolute top-of-the-line limo available was a Rolls-Royce, and that's what I got. When that Rolls pulled up to take me and my new bride away, I thought my father-in-law's jaw would hit the pavement.

"For a comedian, he's not doing so bad," he said to my mother-in-law.

"I always liked him," my mother-in-law said.

We waved at all of our friends and family, ducked the blizzard of confetti that came at us in a downpour, and drove off in the Rolls.

Every honeymoon tells a story. Ours was no exception. Some might even have titles like "Looking for Love in All the Wrong Places," or "Night of the Iguana." Ours was more like "The Road Runner Meets Holiday on Ice."

We decided to honeymoon in Steamboat Springs, Colorado. Gail is by nature a snow bunny. I'm not exactly an Olympic skier, but I know my way around the slopes. Plus, I couldn't let on that I might be less of a skier than she was. It's not that I was competitive with her—Lord knows, I wasn't—but even though we were now married, I still felt I had to impress her. Why? I'm a *guy*.

The second night of our honeymoon we went night skiing. I was schussing here, snowplowing there, showing Gail all my snow moves, which mainly made her laugh, even though I was trying to be cool. We skied down a small ridge and came to a faded sign poking out of the snow that read: DOUBLE BLACK DIAMOND.

"Wow," I said. "A Double Black Diamond ahead."

"What exactly is a Double Black Diamond?"

"I don't know, but it's up ahead."

"Sounds kinda dangerous," Gail said.

"Nah," I said. I drew myself up into my biggest guy pose. "I've never seen a Double Black Diamond before. This could be our only chance to see one. Whatever it is."

"Bill."

To Gail, this was a complete sentence. She didn't have to go beyond "Bill." I knew what the rest of the sentence was without her having to utter another word. The sentence always landed between a warning and a threat, with just a touch of exasperation thrown in for flavor. The rest of the sentence was *Bill, please don't be an idiot and do something stupid that you're gonna regret.*

I didn't listen. As usual.

"Cowabunga!"

I kicked off my spot with my poles, lowered myself into a crouch, and hot-rodded down the hill into the Double Black Diamond.

I'm still not sure what it is. Because within four seconds I came to a steep drop, close to the edge of a cliff. I skidded to a stop, then I tumbled over and began to roll down the hill, head over skis at about a million miles per hour. I tried to call to Gail for help, but my mouth had filled up with snow. I kept rolling, rolling, rolling, until I formed a human snowball.

Finally, I landed at the bottom of the hill. I lay in a heap, flat, immobile. I looked up and on the horizon saw a speck in a ski hat standing at the top of the hill. Gail.

"Bill!"

"Gail," I mumbled. "Double Black Diamond. Way cool."

"BILL!"

I tried to lift myself up, but pain shot across my shoulders. My arms felt as if they had hundred-pound lead weights lashed to each one.

"Are you all right?"

"I'm fine!" I shouted back. "Woo! That was great! Except I can't move my arms!"

"What?"

"I CAN'T MOVE MY ARMS!"

"*Bill.*"

That, too, is a complete sentence.

It means, *Thank God you're alive because now I'm gonna kick your butt for being so stupid.*

She says that one a lot.

I somehow managed to survive the fall and complete the honeymoon without further incident. In fact, we had so much fun the rest of the time in Steamboat that we've made it a tradition to go on at least one vacation a year.

To celebrate our first anniversary, we decided to go to Mexico. Gail had heard about a sailing excursion you could take on a catamaran, just the two of us and a guide. This seemed like a good idea. But I probably should have suspected something when we stepped onto the boat and I introduced us to our guide.

"Hey. I'm Bill, and this is Gail."

"I'm Klaus," the guide said, never taking his eyes off of Gail.

"Klaus," I said. "What part of Mexico you from?"

He stared at me with steel blue Aryan eyes, little swimming pools of terror. "I'm not vrom Mexico. I'm vrom Germany."

"Really? You could never tell."

He turned away from me and put an arm around Gail. "Do you know how to zail a catamaran?"

"No, this is my first time," Gail said.

"Vell, you are zafe vit Klaus." He winked at her. "I hef much experience."

Gail caught my eye. She was trying not to laugh. Her expression said, *Is this guy for real?* I shrugged, found a corner of the catamaran, and decided to drink a beer and enjoy the bazillion dollars we'd spent paying for Klaus and our guided tour.

Klaus steered us out farther and farther from shore. Little beads of sweat started to pop out on his three-ridged forehead, which was the color of cream cheese.

"It eez zo hot," he growled. "Gail, vood you hold za veel?"

"Sure."

Klaus stepped to the side and peeled off his T-shirt. I blinked. He was more cut than Mr. Universe. I had a six-pack at my feet; he had two rippling down his stomach.

"My arms are zo *tight*," he said for no reason, and then for even less reason flexed his biceps. His muscle literally danced.

"Ahhhh," Klaus said. "Better." He patted his stomach, which pinged like a tennis ball hitting the middle of a racket. "Gail, vatch out. You're drifting toward Japan. Let Klaus help you."

Before Gail could move away, Klaus circled his arms around her from behind. Together they steered the catamaran. I shook my head, considering my options. I came up with two: punching him in the head or punching him in the head. Gail, meanwhile, was doing everything she could to stop herself from laughing out loud.

Out of the corner of my eye I saw some water slapping onto the deck of the catamaran. The water became a puddle, and then the puddle rose until it was covering the deck.

"Klaus, I think we're taking on water."

"Vat?" He looked down and saw the water starting to rise even higher. "Oh ya, I zee. Zat is nutting. One time, I vas sailink and za vater came up zo high, a jellyfish came up on za boat."

"No," Gail said.

"Ya," Klaus said. "And you know vat zat jellyfish did?"

"What?"

"He stung me right on my pee-pee."

"Your where?"

"My pee-pee!" And Klaus pointed right to it.

"Did you hear that, Bill?"

"Yep, Gail, his pee-pee. Big owie, huh Klaus?"

Klaus glared at me, his eyes now twin blue lasers. "It svelled up. For *days*."

I thought he was gonna rush me, pick me up, and toss me overboard. Instead he started to bail out the water. Gail started to fake-cough. Otherwise she would've lost it.

"I still haf za scar," Klaus moaned, looking miserably at his private area. "Za end of my pee-pee vas like a balloon."

That did it. Gail burst out laughing, which caused me to do a spit take with my beer.

"Oh, you sink it's vunny?" Klaus said. That amped our laughing up toward redline.

"We're not laughing at you," Gail said.

"No, no, we're laughing with the jellyfish."

"Bill."

There it was. That one word that's really a whole menacing sentence. Except this time it didn't stop me.

"I know. Sorry, Klaus. That was rude. In fact, I feel so bad that I'm gonna make up for it by giving you a huge *tip*."

At that point Gail was laughing so hard that if she'd been pregnant, she would've given birth.

Hell, she was laughing so hard, she almost gave birth anyway.

37. TEXAS BIG HAIR

When you look at Gail and me on paper, you couldn't find two people who seem more unsuited for each other. I bet if we signed up for a dating service, the computer would spit us out before it matched us up. The two of us are like night and day.

She's practical. I'm not.

She's got common sense. I don't.

She's logical and careful. I'm not.

She thinks things through. I don't.

She likes to do a ton of research. I like to wing it.

Bottom line: I'm a guy. She's not. She's definitely not.

With all these differences, you might wonder how we've managed to stay married for almost twenty-five years. I can tell you in two words:

We laugh.

We crack each other up and we find the same things funny. Mainly, we see the world in the same silly and sometimes twisted way. Laughing has gotten us through our hardest times. If we hadn't been able to laugh at life and ourselves, I think we would've killed each other.

It doesn't take a big elaborate joke. The littlest things can set us off for hours.

On the plane ride back from our Mexico trip, Gail and I were sitting in coach behind a woman who had what we call Texas Big Hair. It appeared that she'd had her entire head permed into a big pale blue tower. It looked like someone had dipped her upside down into a vat of cotton candy. Every time she moved her head, her hair would wobble and sway and move in the opposite direction, like it was alive.

"She's got cartoon hair," Gail whispered.

"She does. She looks like Marge Simpson."

Did she think it looked good? And did she think hair actually came in that color? I've heard of brown, black, yellow, red, gray, and white. Those are your choices. Never heard of blue. Because hair does not come in that color. When you look at hair dye manufacturers, you do not see the name Crayola.

I shook my head and started flipping through the in-flight magazine while Gail pulled out a tube of hand lotion. She started to ask me a question. She squeezed the tube and—

Squirrrrrrrrrt!

A glob of hand lotion shot out of the tube, flew into the back of the woman's big blue hair, and stuck there, *splat*, forming a white cakey clump.

The woman never moved. Didn't feel a thing.

Gail and I stared at the blob of white goo fastened to the back of her hair, and we started laughing uncontrollably. I fell into that zone of dangerous laughter where the tears fly out fast and furious and you literally can't catch your breath. I thought I was going to fall over into the aisle and knock over the beverage cart.

Gail whispered, "Do we tell her?"

"Yeah, good idea," I said. "I'll tell her."

I didn't move.

"Well?"

"I'm just trying to figure out what to say. 'Excuse me, ma'am. You have a wad of white goo stuck in the back of your big hair.'"

Gail paused and mulled this over. "Maybe we should let it be."

"Yeah. She'll find out sooner or later. Like in a month. When she gets her hair repainted at Earl Scheib."

We started up again. This time I was doubled over, laughing so hard that my stomach hurt.

To be honest, I didn't think that being married to Gail would be that much different from living with her. I was wrong. It was better. Can't say exactly how. It just was. It wasn't that being married made us legal. It was more like we'd now made a contract with each other, an unconditional commitment. Gail and I are as different as two people can be, but there is one quality we share. We're both loyal to a fault. We knew that once we said, "I do," nobody was going anywhere. No matter what.

For the first year of our marriage, we stayed in Dallas and went on living the life of comedian and normal person. I continued my job

as emcee at the comedy club, where I barely eked out a living. I justi-
fied not making any money by saying to both Gail and myself that I
loved what I did and I was paying my dues.

Gail soon saw that I was clueless when it came to our finances. I
couldn't balance a checkbook and didn't grasp the concept of saving.
I believed that a penny earned was a penny to spend, as long as you
spent it on the necessities of life: a really good TV, a pantry full of
nourishing food like potato chips and jerky, plenty of beer, and my
very own La-Z-Boy chair. Gail had this harebrained idea that we
should put our money in a bank and save it. Somehow she did it.
I don't know how, but even with our two meager salaries, she managed to squirrel away a little bit here, a little there, and slowly, me-
thodically, our savings account began to grow.

This was great because I was saving up for something we desperately needed.

A boat.

Every time I mentioned that I wanted a boat, Gail would roll her
eyes and say, "Bill, where are we going to get the money?"

"It doesn't have to be a fifty-foot yacht. I want something small.
I've got my eye on the want ads."

"Well, all right. We'll do some research."

In a few months, our savings account was bulging with a balance
of over a thousand dollars.

"We got enough money now," I said.

"Where you gonna find a boat for under a thousand dollars?" Gail
asked.

"Right here." I slapped the open page of the classified ads. I had
found an ad for a motorboat, with water skis and a trailer, all for eight
hundred dollars.

"Bill, eight hundred dollars? I don't know—"

"Gail, this thing's gonna go. If we don't act now, we're gonna
lose it."

"I'd just like to do some research."

"Here's my research. It's a boat. It's eight hundred dollars. Let's buy it. Please. I want a boat so *bad*."

I admit it. I can be a child.

But it worked. Because before you could say "Captain Jack Sparrow," we were standing in the backyard outside a small house in a suburb of Dallas, talking to Cal, the boat's owner. He was running his hand lovingly along the side of an old wooden speedboat. I suppose some ignorant people might call it a glorified dinghy.

"This here's my baby," Cal said, his eyes welling up with tears. "Kills me to sell her."

"So why are you?" Gail asked, her hands on her hips, her head tilted to one side. Translated: She wasn't buying a word of Cal's sob story.

"Need the money." Cal sniffed.

"I can relate," I said. "Money's tight."

"I hear *that*," said Cal.

I took a slow stroll around the boat. I have no idea why. I had no idea what I was looking for. If the boat had tires, I would've kicked them. I scratched my chin.

"Eight hundred, huh?"

"Yep. And that, my friend, is a steal."

I looked at the boat. It was jet black and had fins.

"Does the boat come with a motor?" Gail asked.

"You bet," Cal said. "Evinrude. The best."

I looked at Gail. She rolled her eyes, a signal that said, *This guy's full of crap. Let's get outta here, go home, and do more research.*

"I'm not buying it until I see the motor," I said.

"I wouldn't sell it to you until you see the motor," Cal said, and limped toward a shed. I hadn't noticed his limp before. I wasn't sure whether it was real and had just started to kick up or it was fake and he just remembered it.

After a minute, he came out of the shed wheeling an outboard motor in a wheelbarrow. Cal dragged a garden hose over toward us and filled up a trashcan with water. We lifted the motor into the trashcan and submerged it in the water. Cal pulled the choke, and after only two tries, the motor hummed to life.

"She'll do forty-five without breaking a sweat," he shouted over the roar of the outboard.

"Sold," I said.

"Bill, shouldn't we take the boat out on the lake?" Gail said, squeezing my arm in alarm.

"Nah. Water is water, whether it's in a lake or a trashcan, right, Cal?"

"You said it."

"You take Visa?" I said, watching Cal's face turn snow white. "Just kidding."

I pulled eight one-hundred-dollar bills out of my shirt pocket.

"Take good care of her," Cal said, snatching the bills away.

"That boat is really unattractive," Gail said on the way home.

"It has character," I said.

"I call that ugly."

We'd stopped at U-Haul on the way to Cal's, and we were now towing our new boat home. I couldn't stop beaming.

"I own a boat," I said.

"Congratulations," Gail said without meaning it.

"You don't understand," I said. "A man is not officially a man until he owns a boat."

"Where do you get that?"

"It's a known fact."

"None of my boyfriends ever owned a boat," she said.

"I rest my case," I said.

Gail shook her head and sighed. "What are we gonna name her?"

"What?"

"Every boat has a name."

"Bat Boat," I said.

"Catchy."

"You don't like it?"

"Not much."

"Okay, you name her," I said.

"Oh, I have a name. It's three words. And the first two are 'Piece of.'"

"Quiet," I whispered. "Bat Boat might hear you. She's very sensitive."

We scheduled Bat Boat's maiden voyage for the following Saturday morning. Gail, my buddy Rick, and I loaded a bag of sandwiches, a cooler of beer, and the water skis into the hull. By this time, Gail had gotten with the program. She knew Bat Boat wasn't the prettiest vessel in the harbor, but she was ours, and Gail had accepted her as a member of our family.

"Man, this is one ugly boat," Rick said, climbing in.

"That's why I love her," Gail said.

"Oh, now you love her?" I said.

"I'm her mama."

"I love you," I said, and kissed her.

"Can you two not do that?" Rick said. "I feel like a third testicle."

I stood up in the rear of Bat Boat and pulled the engine's choke cord. Again after just two tries, the motor kicked in.

"Listen to that baby *sing*," I shouted above the engine's roar.

"Awesome," Rick said.

"It's a miracle," Gail said.

We putt-putted around the lake for a while, drinking beer, catching rays, basking in the wonder of my new Bat Boat.

"This is the best," I said.

"I'm jealous of you, man," Rick said. "Every guy should have a boat."

He raised his beer to me. I beamed. Gail beamed and raised her beer, too.

"Let's break out the water skis," Rick said.

"Woo-hoo!" I shouted.

"It's your boat. You're up first," Rick said. "I'll pull you."

With Gail at the helm, Bat Boat glided toward shore. Gail cut the motor, and the boat drifted a few more feet and stopped. I hopped out. Rick handed me the water skis, and I slipped them on. Rick tossed me the rope; I caught it and got into a crouch.

"Ready?"

"Let 'er rip!"

Gail sat down and gripped the sides of Bat Boat for support. Rick yanked the motor's choke cord.

Nothing.

He yanked again, harder.

Still nothing.

He looked at Gail. Gail shrugged.

With both hands, Rick pulled the choke with all his might. The engine growled, made a disturbing grinding noise, turned over, and began to shriek. The boat lurched forward, hauling me up on the skis. The engine suddenly rose into a high-pitched, ear-shattering squeal, wheezed a cloud of black smoke, and died.

Then the right side of Bat Boat fell into the water. Gail leaned both hands onto the left side. The side collapsed and she fell into the water.

"Throw her a life preserver!" I shouted to Rick.

"There is none!" He looked frantically for something to throw toward Gail, something to grab onto. He spotted the one thing that was sure to float.

The cooler.

He lifted it with both hands and prepared to toss it overboard.

"Not the beer!" I shouted.

"Bill!" Gail screamed. Her head disappeared below the surface. Her arms shot up, flailing frantically—and then they stopped and sank.

Gail abruptly stood up, her hands fastened on her hips. The water was barely up to her waist. She'd fallen into three feet of water. She started walking toward me. She wagged a threatening finger at me. "I don't believe it. You wouldn't throw the cooler overboard to save your *wife?"*

"Gail, it was filled with imported beer. If it was Bud or Coors—"

"Run for your life," Rick said. I tried, but I had on the water skis and I couldn't move. Within seconds Gail was next to me, trying to look upset, failing because she was laughing hysterically. She shoved me in the chest and I tumbled backward into the lake, nearly impaling myself on the water skis.

An hour later the Coast Guard arrived and towed the remains of Bat Boat back to the dock. We found a boat mechanic with a shop nearby who assessed the damage, clicking his tongue the whole time he gave Bat Boat the once-over.

"Where'd you find this beauty?"

"Ask the captain," Gail said, nodding at me.

"Every man's gotta have a boat, right?" I said. The mechanic just shrugged.

"How much will it cost to fix it?" Gail, always practical, asked.

"Fix it? I don't think so. They don't even make parts for this model anymore. I think this is a '52."

I was stunned. "This boat was built in 1952?"

"Thereabouts," the mechanic said.

"Gail, we bought a classic." I turned to the mechanic. "Give me your best guess. How much is she worth? Round figures."

The mechanic shrugged. "Maybe fifty."

"Fifty *grand?"*

"Fifty dollars."

Gail turned and headed toward the car.

"Gail!" I called after her.

The mechanic rocked back on his heels. "She don't look too happy."

"A death in her family," I explained, then paused. "Me."

I haven't owned a boat since.

38. SCREAM

The months went by in Dallas. I kept working at my comedy, sharpening and expanding my standup and honing my emceeing. As I celebrated my one-year anniversary at the club and headed into year two, I started to realize something kind of shocking: I didn't actually suck.

I started to build a reputation. Most people lined up to see the headliners, but I developed a following, too. I had a fan base that consisted of several people, even beyond Gail and my in-laws. Then Gail and I started talking seriously about my career. She was the one who actually made the radical suggestion.

"Bill, if you're gonna have even a chance to make it, we have to move. You have to be in L.A."

Of course, she was right. L.A. is the center of the entertainment universe. I had gone as far as I could in Dallas.

"How much time will you give me?" I asked her.

"As long as you need," Gail said.

"How's this? In ten years, if I'm still emceeing comedy clubs and picking up headliners at the airport and then dropping off their dry cleaning, we can either move back to Dallas or you can shoot me. Your choice."

Gail smiled. "Deal."

So we got ready to seek fame and fortune on the Left Coast, in La La Land, where comedy was king.

We packed up all our earthly belongings, said adios to the great state of Texas, and moved . . . to Kansas City.

Got a job offer I couldn't refuse: working in a comedy club and living rent free in the owner's basement, which actually was a lot nicer than it sounds.

So we took a little detour from our life in L.A. and settled for a time in the Midwest.

Turned out to be a great move. The owner and his family took us in like a couple of strays and basically adopted us. Meanwhile, I got to improve my comedy even more, building up my confidence, if not our savings. Finally, Gail and I decided it was time. I was ready.

We moved to L.A. with the wind at our backs.

We didn't know a soul. Didn't have a dime. Had no idea what we were doing. Found a great little house in Santa Monica that we couldn't afford.

Soon after we moved in, I put two and two together and figured out that all the uncertainty was getting to Gail. I could tell because she started throwing up about every five minutes. One day, after Gail endured a particularly nasty bout of what's known in the medical profession as major league hurling, I figured out what was wrong with her.

"You gotta give up Mexican food," I said.

"You idiot," she said. "I'm pregnant."

"*What?*"

"I'm having your baby."

"Are you kidding me? Wow! *She's having my baby. What a lovely way to say that she really loves me. She's having my—*"

"Bill."

"Sorry, honey. When?"

"I'm only a few weeks."

"No, I meant when do you think you conceived? Was it that night on the beach? You know, I think that lifeguard saw us. Nah, it was probably after that party, with the incense and the candles. Wait. Was it halftime during the Cowboys-Giants game? When we ran out of beer? Wouldn't that be awesome? Our kid is gonna be a Cowboys fan—"

"*Bill.*"

"Sorry." I slipped my arms around her waist and kissed her. "Honey, I am really happy."

"Me, too."

"You're gonna be the best mother ever," I said.

"And you're gonna be a father."

She grinned, leaned up and kissed me. I nuzzled her neck.

Then she threw up in the wastebasket.

Gail survived morning sickness, or in her case, morning, noon, and night sickness, and sailed into her second trimester. The more weight she gained, the more beautiful she became. It was as if there were always a light shining around her, a twenty-four-hour spotlight. She made me forget that making a living as a comedian is a risky business. She just has a way. Gail taught me to take each day as it comes, not to fret over the little things.

We still laughed, too. All the time.

One night, when Gail was about seven months pregnant, we decided to go out to dinner. Our house was unusual for Santa Monica because we had a screened-in front porch. We never kept the outside door, the screen door, locked. Matter of fact, we rarely kept the inside door locked, either. Don't know why. We just never thought about it. To top it off, the doorbell didn't work. Bottom line, you could open the screen door, walk across the front porch, come inside our house, open the fridge, grab a beer, turn on the TV, and settle in on the couch without ever knocking or ringing the doorbell.

"With a kid on the way, you ought to fix the doorbell," Gail said as we were heading out.

"I'm on it. This weekend. Right after the Angels game. And NASCAR. And the Country Music Awards."

"Bill. This is serious."

"I will. I really will."

Gail rolled her eyes. I turned my back to the porch and give her my most sincere trust-me smile.

"I promise. Saturday. Right after my nap. No. Before my nap. How's that?"

I reached for the doorknob, opened the door from our house to the porch, and found myself face-to-face with a large, scraggly-looking guy. A stranger. Standing on the porch.

I screamed.

A full-blown freaked-out rip-your-head-off primitive banshee wail.

"AHHHHHHHHHHHHHHHHH!" I howled.

"AHHHHHHHHHHHHHHHHH!" the guy howled.

"AHHHHHHHHHHHHHHHHH!" I howled again, backed up, and nearly knocked Gail over.

Then I grinned like an idiot and tried to ignore what had just happened.

"Hey," I said.

"Your doorbell doesn't work," the guy said.

"Yeah," I said. "It just broke. Gonna fix it this weekend. Right after my nap. Before. Before my nap."

The guy nodded nervously. I realized now that he was completely freaked out. More freaked out than I was. If that was possible.

"Is Bob here?" the guy asked.

"Nope. No Bob." I paused. I'd just made a total fool out of myself. Might as well go all the way. I narrowed my eyes into slits and channeled Jack Nicholson in *The Shining*.

"Who the hell is *Bob?*" I said.

"He must've moved," the guy said. "No worries." He turned and ran off the porch and disappeared down the street. I watched him go, still weirded out. Suddenly, I heard a cackling sound behind me. I turned and saw Gail doubled over, tears streaking down her cheeks.

"Gail. Oh my God."

But then I saw that she wasn't in pain; she was laughing hysterically.

"Oh no," she managed to say between laughs. "I'm laughing so hard, I think my water's gonna break."

"Hold on. I'll get a bucket to catch it."

"That poor guy," she said. "He thought you were a total nut bag."

"Him? What about me?"

"Fix the doorbell," she said.

Still laughing, she waddled past me toward the car.

39. QUALITY TIME

There are rules about being a guy. You can look 'em up in the manual.

You didn't know there was a manual? You must not be a guy.

Oh, the manual hasn't been written down. You can't buy it in a bookstore or at Wal-Mart. Don't need to. The manual is implanted in every guy's brain the day he's born. It's just there. If you're a guy, you know what I'm talking about.

You also know that Rule Number One is: *Guys do not cry.* The only exception is if a player is on the team that wins the World Series or the NBA Championship. Or during the end of *Field of Dreams.*

I break this rule all the time. Can't help it. As we've discussed, I cry. A lot. I try not to. I try to hold back the tears. I cough, swallow, and picture disgusting things, happy things, silly things. Nothing helps. I'm thinking of getting some guy cry therapy.

When Gail gave birth to our daughter Emily, I cried an ocean. I couldn't believe that in the matter of one second, Gail and I went from being this goofy married couple to being a *family*. Just like that. Here was this tiny person, looking up at me through her gorgeous filmy eyes, not even able to focus yet, and I knew right then that everything else in my life had fallen into second place. I'd just met Emily and I would have given my life for her. Little did I realize that over the course of the next eighteen years I'd also give her several million dollars, some of which she'd use for college, most of which she'd use to buy shoes.

When Emily was born, I cried constantly. Cried when I held her. Cried when she cried. Cried when I strolled her around the block. Cried when I changed her.

I'm gonna let you in on a secret right now. Boy babies are not the only ones who can squirt you with a stream from their little private hoses. I don't know the mechanism little girl babies have going, but I foolishly thought that when I changed her I was out of danger.

Wrong. Got hit right in the eye. *Whap.* Stunned me. Had no time to duck. "Ooh, Emily got Daddy good! Ha ha ha. Wow."

Then I started to cry because I thought it was so cute getting squirted in the eye by my daughter's pee.

I actually had good reason to cry when Emily was a baby, because by then I'd started playing clubs all around the country and I was on the road a lot. Sometimes I'd be gone four weeks at a time. When I first got the gigs, I was excited because it meant I was starting to make it as a comedian. Then the road started to wear on me. Not just the travel but the loneliness. I would play a club, then spend the night in some fleabag motel, longing to be with Gail as she got closer and closer to giving birth. I began to wonder if our baby would even recognize me. Then I got an idea. I heard about it on TV. I made a tape of my voice and I had Gail play it and hold it close to her stomach so Emily could hear it in utero. I didn't say anything earth-shattering, just "Hey, Emily, this is Daddy. I'm working now, but I'll see you soon. I love you."

I think it worked, because the first time I held Emily, I said, "Hey, Emily, this is Daddy. I love you," and she smiled up at the sound of my voice.

Man, did I cry. A nurse came running over, thinking there was something wrong.

"Everything's fine," I blubbered. "My daughter recognized my voice. She *smiled* at me."

The nurse sighed in relief, then muttered under her breath, "The baby has gas."

"No," I said loudly. "She recognized my *voice*. I don't smile when I have gas. Do you?"

She looked at me like I was a mental patient, then hustled out of there.

The worst part of being on the road was when I started missing stuff. Landmarks. The first time Emily rolled over. Her first step. Her first word, which was, of course, "Dada."

I didn't cry much when Gail told me that. Yeah, right. Noah saw less water.

Being on the road, missing some of the highlights of watching my kids grow up, did have one positive result. My time at home was quality time. I know that phrase gets tossed around a lot, but in my case it was true. I couldn't wait to get home and hang out with my family. When I was home, I was *there*. I know a lot of guys come home from work at the end of the day and instead of being with their family or loved ones, they pound back a few beers and vegetate in front of the TV. Same thing on the weekends. They're sitting in their living rooms, but their minds are somewhere else. Not me. When I walked in that door from being on the road, I felt as if I had to make up for lost time. I got involved.

I think it was actually worse for me than for my kids. My being on the road was their reality. It was what they'd always known. I didn't give them something and then take it away. I remember when my son Travis was eight or nine, we were shooting hoops in the driveway. We were horsing around, having a great time. All of a sudden I looked at him and I got teary-eyed.

"What's wrong, Dad?"

"I want to apologize to you," I said.

"For what?"

"For not being here for you all the time." He looked at me blankly. "I'm going on the road again tomorrow. I'll be gone for two weeks. I'm sorry."

"It's not like tomorrow's the first time you're ever going on the road," Travis said, and then he shrugged. "We'll hang out when you get back."

That's when I realized that my kids were used to me being away and that, to them, it really wasn't a big deal. I was the one who was guilty. *Get over it*, said the little voice in my head. *They're fine.*

I tried—but of course I never would get over it.

So to make up for being gone, I'd go all out when I was home, especially on holidays. I love holidays, every one of 'em. One Easter I hid eggs and candy all over the house and yard. Emily was four or five and she'd been waiting to go Easter egg and candy hunting for two weeks. She slept with her Easter basket. At the time, the candy of choice was Whoppers, which were little malted milk balls that came in tiny milk cartons. I hid a whole basket full of Whoppers in the living room. Emily found it and her whole face lit up.

"Look!" she said, running over to me with excitement. "The Easter Bunny gave us milk!"

Halloween is my favorite holiday. I pretty much go nuts every year. I don't get why kids should have all the fun. Some kids, the older ones, take Halloween for granted. They don't even go trick-or-treating. They just show up at your door dressed in street clothes. No attempt at a costume. They figure you ring the doorbell and, boom, free candy.

No.

It doesn't work that way at my house. You gotta earn it. Or at least pretend that you're trying.

For several years in a row, I got dressed up as Dracula. I didn't stop there. I turned the front yard into a graveyard dotted with Styrofoam headstones. I also planted several rubber hands that stuck up out of the ground. I strung lights that I programmed to go on and off, an attempt to create an eerie lightning effect. Then I made a tape of Halloween songs punctuated with me cackling, doing an uncanny impression of Count Dracula, at least in my mind.

Finally, I built a coffin. For Gail. She put on a Bride of Dracula costume, slapped on a coat of ghost-white makeup, lay down inside the coffin, and pretended to be dead. When kids came to the door for candy, I'd walk out of the house as Dracula, give them my most frightening look, and say in my terrible Transylvanian accent, "I hef no candy. So I vil haf to bite your neck and zuck your blood." At that point, Gail would suddenly sit up in the coffin and offer a cauldron filled with candy bars. The kids loved it.

The year Gail was pregnant with Emily, she obviously couldn't lie down in the coffin. The kids were upset. One kid blurted out, "Where's the lady in the coffin?"

I didn't know it at the time, but that kid very nearly saw the future.

40. BLOOD SIMPLE

Whenever I was with Emily, people would stop me and say, "Oh, she's so beautiful. Who does she look like? Your wife?"

What was I supposed to say to that?

Yep. She looks just like Gail. Thank God. Because if she looked like me, you'd start screaming, make the sign of the cross, and run like hell.

Or . . .

She might look like Gail, but she definitely has my personality. Because she's easy to live with.

Emily did take after me in one unfortunate way. She always seemed to land in the hospital.

The first and most serious time occurred when she was three months old. Emily had been born with a slight dimple in the middle of her back. We ran some tests, and the doctors concluded that she actually had a stalk that was connected to her spinal cord.

"Nothing may ever happen," the doctor said.

"That's great. What a relief," I said.

"Or she could trip and fall and be paralyzed for the rest of her life."

As a parent, what do you do? Kids fall all the time. Gail and I talked it through, analyzed it from every angle, then realized that we had no choice. She had to have the surgery.

The day she was going to have the operation was just hell. I'd been on the road for four weeks and I was a wreck. There's nothing better for comedy than thinking about your little baby going in for back surgery.

Somehow I got through it and flew home in time for the surgery. We stayed by Emily's side until it was time to wheel her down to the operating room. I held one of her hands, Gail held the other. Emily was too young to know what was going on, which was the one saving grace. We came off the elevator, and the surgeon was waiting for us.

"We'll take her from here," he said.

"How long do you think the operation will take?" I asked.

"I'm anticipating eight hours."

A whole workday. Unfathomable.

The doctor took the gurney and wheeled her away from us. Gail and I stood watching helplessly, gripping each other's hands.

My dad and stepmother and Gail's mom had flown in. Gail and I met them downstairs in the waiting room.

"Look, you guys have to eat something," Dad said. "Let's go across the street to the hotel. They got a breakfast buffet."

I didn't feel like eating, but with eight hours to kill, there didn't seem to be much else to do. Gail and I walked over to the hotel like a

doctor went to work. But Emily shrieked and gripped my hand and the doctor said, "Hold her head while I stitch her up."

"Roger," I said. Don't remember much after that. I held Emily's head, she screamed a lot, the doctor worked quickly like an expert seamstress, thread was flying, and then, amazingly, he was done.

"You did great," he said.

"Thanks," I said. "I really thought I was gonna lose it."

"I was talking to Emily," he said.

I know. What a guy. I pass out at the sight of blood and cry at Cialis commercials. Adds up to low grades on the Guy Scale. You would think. But you'd be wrong.

Because being able to admit your weaknesses makes you *more* of a guy. Really.

It's in the manual.

41. JUST A MAN

Gail is such a loving, nurturing person that I always assumed we'd have a herd of kids because she's the world's greatest mother. We're talking Moms Hall of Fame, first ballot. Only thing is, after Emily, she just couldn't seem to stay pregnant. She got pregnant a few times, but then she'd have a miscarriage. Losing a baby was awful. But then we'd gear up and try again. That part I enjoyed.

One time, when we were living in Santa Monica, Gail went through a difficult miscarriage. We were young and not that sophisticated medically, but the way I understood it, the way the doctor explained it, Gail had lost a tube. She used to have two tubes, and now she only had one.

What we didn't know was that she'd had twins. One was in utero, the other was still in the tube.

The ultrasound didn't show two tubes. It only showed one. After the miscarriage, the doctor pronounced Gail was "clean." Except that Gail was still feeling funky. We went back and had another ultrasound. He looked at it, nodded, and said, "Yeah, it's clean."

I'm not a doctor, that's obvious, but I thought I saw something on the X-ray. I pointed at it. "What's that?"

The doctor peered at it, studied it for a couple of seconds, and said, "Probably just a cyst. Nothing to worry about."

Of course, what nobody knew was that I was looking right at the other baby, the twin, growing inside her second tube. The invisible tube.

It was Christmas week, and we'd planned a family trip to Abilene to visit my mom. On the day after Christmas, Emily, who was three, Gail, and I were hanging around the living room. Gail hadn't said much all morning. She'd still been feeling under the weather since we'd arrived in Abilene. That morning she just seemed out of it. She looked kind of pale, and her eyes had a distant, almost vacant look. Totally unlike her. At one point, she excused herself and went to the bathroom. I played with Emily, chased her around, did my usual goofy Daddy "You can't catch me" game, the one where I let her catch me so I could grab her and tickle her until we were both laughing helplessly. In the middle of the game, Gail called me from the bathroom. Her voice was small and weak and urgent. I handed Emily off to my mother and went into the bathroom.

Gail was lying on the floor. She was white. She could barely speak. "I'm in so much pain," she said.

"Show me where."

She bit her lip and cradled her stomach. Tears started dripping down her cheeks.

I helped her to her feet, a struggle, and out of the bathroom. I took my mom aside and told her that I was taking Gail to the hospital. Then I told Emily that we'd be back soon, trying to cover up how worried I was. Even at three, Emily knew something was going on.

"Mommy's gonna be fine," I said. "We'll be back before you know it." It took everything I had not to break down in front of her. I didn't know what was happening, but I knew this much: It wasn't good.

I got Gail out to the driveway and somehow got her into the car. I floored it and drove her to the hospital in Abilene. When we pulled into the hospital's emergency room driveway, shaped like a horseshoe, Gail said, her voice a thin click, "I was born in this hospital."

I didn't know what to make of her saying that. Every moment of that day felt magnified, and everything that was happening felt as if it were unfolding either in super slow motion or at warp speed.

The ER was small, and there were only a few patients. One was a guy who was in the middle of dying of a heart attack. A few of the staff were paying close attention to him. The rest were focused on a woman with a sore throat who was screaming as if she had a fork stuck in her neck. The Squeaky Wheel Theory at work.

I led Gail to the admitting window. She was hunched over, in a world of pain. After we finished filling out the paperwork, I steered her over to a chair in the waiting room. She could barely sit. She squelched a full-out scream because she didn't want to draw attention to herself. It wouldn't have mattered, because she would've been drowned out by the woman with the sore throat anyway. With my help, she lowered herself onto a couch. Once she was lying down, the pain subsided. Gail clutched a pillow and closed her eyes. We waited, and waited, and waited some more.

After what seemed like a year, an intern came in. He stopped and looked around the room. By then the old guy had been buried, and I'd bound and gagged the lady with the sore throat and tossed her into a supply closet.

"Mrs. Engvall?" the intern said.

"So soon?" I said.

Gail sat up, and instantly pain engulfed her abdomen. She tried not to scream and instead took a divot out of my arm with her fingernails. The intern brought us into a small, curtain-enclosed area and took her vitals. He was young and well-meaning and clueless. All that we could establish was that when Gail was lying down, she was okay. The moment she sat up, her pain went through the roof.

"Huh," the intern said, jotting down some notes on a clipboard.

"Yeah, that's as far as I got, too," I said. Even in her condition, Gail shot me a look. I didn't care. I was angry and scared, and I wanted to know what was going on with my wife.

"I'm just taking down information," the intern said. "We're going to take your blood pressure, run some other tests, and by the process of elimination we'll determine the nature of your discomfort and the proper protocol."

In other words, *I have no idea what's wrong with her.*

He had Gail sit up and took her blood pressure. She bit her lip to try to deal with her excruciating pain. He scribbled some numbers on a clipboard, and I sneaked a look: 60 over 10. In medical terms that means *Holy crap.*

The intern asked some more questions. I told him all about Gail's recent miscarriage. That caused him to raise an eyebrow. He wrote something else on the clipboard, then excused himself to phone the ob-gyn who was on call.

As the intern left the room, Gail lowered herself back onto the gurney. She stared at the ceiling. I held her hand and watched her eyes. She seemed fixated on something far away. I was now beyond scared, beyond pissed. I felt completely helpless and useless. I wanted to hug her, I wanted to make her laugh, I wanted this to be a bad dream . . .

———

D r. Cass was about to sit down for Christmas dinner when he got the call. His family had come in from out of town. He lived for these occasions. Holidays were one of the few times now that brought his whole family together.

He moved into the hallway to answer the phone. It was the hospital. The intern explained what was going on. He referred to his notes on the clipboard. He was new and unsure. Dr. Cass listened carefully and glanced at his family gathered around the dining room table.

The intern finished reading from his clipboard. Dr. Cass ran a hand through his thick hair. "Keep an eye on her," he said, and hung up the phone.

He started to walk into the dining room to join his family. He got halfway there and stopped in the middle of the hallway. He felt a chill run through him. His wife saw him standing in the hall and walked over to him.

"Are you okay?"

"I have to go to the hospital," Dr. Cass said. "I'm sorry."

His wife said nothing. She understood.

Then Dr. Cass said, "I don't know why, but I have to see this woman."

F ifteen minutes later, Dr. Cass was standing over Gail, taking her blood pressure. He wasn't an older man, but his eyes were soft and full of wisdom. He nodded once, then looked at me. Without a word, he grabbed the gurney, spun it around, and raced down the hallway toward the operating room. He turned and shouted over his shoulder, "Let's go! Now! We may need blood!"

Everything started swirling around me. It was as if I were in the middle of a psychedelic dream: lights blinking, doors slamming, disconnected voices shouting, a swarm of people in green scrubs brushing past me. I tried to ask questions, but nobody could hear me. Then Gail was gone, in surgery, and I was alone.

I wandered into an empty hospital room just off the nurse's station and called my dad. In a daze, I explained what was going on as best I could. He listened carefully and in a calm, soothing voice, in contrast to the turmoil that I was feeling, said, "Sounds like she's bleeding internally. There might have been another tube that didn't show up in the ultrasound."

It was amazing to me that he could piece together exactly what Gail was going through with the bits of garbled information I'd given him. It was even more amazing that this was happening at all. Gail was young and beautiful, inside and out. She, of all people, did not deserve anything like this.

"Dad," I said, "I don't know what to do. Tell me what to do."

"There's nothing you can do." He hesitated, and then he said: "You just gotta be the man."

Be the man.

I wanted to tell him that I was just a guy. I wasn't ready to be the man.

Then, for the briefest moment, my life passed before my eyes. But it wasn't my whole life. It was just the bad parts. Struggling to make it as a comic. Constantly being on the road. Doing my show and crashing in some fleabag motel miles away from anyone I knew. Trying to be a dad to a three-year-old. And now this. *What if Gail—*

What if—

I sighed heavily. I was exhausted. "I don't know if I can handle this." Dad said nothing.

"This wasn't in the manual," I said. "This kind of stuff. It ain't there."

"Nope," he said.

We stayed on the phone, not talking, just listening to each other breathe. That's all I needed at that moment, just to hear my dad breathe . . .

I looked up and Dr. Cass was standing in the doorway. He was smiling.

"She's gonna be fine," he said. "We had to take out six pints of blood, but we got it tied off. She's fine now. Just fine."

"What happened?"

He confirmed what we all thought. "There was a second tube. Nobody knew about it. It burst. When Gail was lying down, her blood pressure stabilized. The moment she sat up, her blood pressure plummeted."

"There was another tube—"

"Yeah. There was another baby and it grew and the tube broke. But she's fine now."

I heard myself say, "Was it close?"

"It was close," he said softly. "Real close."

I swallowed. "What can I do?"

"Nothing. She's sleeping. Gonna be out for a while. Go home and get some rest. You're worn out."

I muttered a muffled "Thanks," and I shook his hand and then I saw the phone dangling. "Dad?" I said into the receiver.

"I'm here. I'm still here." The deepest, truest words I'd ever heard.

"You were right," I said.

"Can I talk to the doctor?"

I handed the phone to Dr. Cass, and as he and my dad spoke, I stumbled out of the empty hospital and into the hall. I stared at the swinging doors that led into the operating rooms, and my entire body shivered.

She's okay, I thought. *She's okay.*

Now I needed to see Emily.

My mom and Emily were waiting for me. I scooped Emily up in my arms.

"It's late," I said. "You have to get ready for bed."

I swung her up on my shoulders and carried her piggyback into her bedroom. I dumped her onto her bed, and she giggled, and then she said, "Where's Mommy?"

For the first time that day I cried.

It all came out. All the fear and worry over the possibility of losing Gail. It rushed out like a dam bursting. Then I sobbed because I was so happy. I was so happy that I could say, "Mommy's sick. She's just sick. She's gonna be home soon," and that I didn't have to say, "Mommy's gone to see God."

Then I lay down on the bed next to Emily and held her. We didn't say another word, because we both knew it was going to be all right.

Weeks later, when Gail was out of the woods and recovering at home, she called that day her "re-birthday."

"I like that," I said. And then I paused. "Did you ever feel that you were gonna, you know—"

"No. I never felt like I was gonna die. Never. I just kept thinking that I was born in this hospital, no way I'm gonna die here. No way."

Close. Real close.

L ife is full of trauma and tragedy. Even when you're a kid, you know it, but most of the time that stuff seems off in the distance, out of reach. You figure the adults in your life will handle it because they're *adults* and they know what they're doing.

That's the biggest myth going. We don't know what we're doing. Half the time we stumble through life as if we're wearing blindfolds.

My dad was right. At the worst times, like when Gail was in danger of dying, you have to stop being just a guy and you have to be a man. And there really should be a "How to" manual to help us through. After all, the word "man" is in "manual." No such thing as a "guyual."

I pinpoint that day as the day I became a man. I'm still a guy, always was, always will be, but now I know what being a man means. Found that out in that hospital in Abilene.

Being a man has nothing to do with being strong or tough. Being a man doesn't mean you have to solve every problem. Not it at all.

Being a man means that those closest to you can count on you.

It's like when Yul Brynner asks Steve McQueen to join up with him in *The Magnificent Seven*.

"How many men you got?" Steve asks Yul.

Yul smiles and holds up one finger.

Steve smiles back and holds up two fingers.

I'm holding up a finger right now. Yul can count on me, too. And so can my family and friends.

P.S. About ten years after Gail went through her "re-birthday," I happened to be working in Abilene, doing a show at a local comedy club. As soon as I checked into the hotel, I looked up Dr. Cass's number and called him.

"Don't know if you remember me. My name is Bill Engvall."

"I remember your wife," he said. "We almost lost her."

Well, of course, I got choked up. I said, "Dr. Cass, you tell everybody in your office that there are free tickets waiting for them at Will Call."

"You don't have to do that," he said.

"Yes, I do," I said. "It's the least I have to do."

42. BRA SHOPPING

Zap. Fast forward to today. Feels like I've been riding a bullet train. Twenty years here and gone in the blink of an eye. Emily's in college, and our son, Travis, our miracle child because I never thought we'd have another baby, is in high school, driving me crazy because he, too, is just a guy.

My career, thanks to a lot of hardworking people and a ton of luck, hit overdrive. I played the club circuit all over the country, got "discovered," did the *Tonight Show* with Johnny Carson (the sweetest sound to a comedian was the sound of Johnny laughing), won the American Comedy

Awards Standup Comic of the Year in 1992, then *Delta,* the Blue Collar Comedy Tour, movies, TV show, specials, Vegas, concerts.

And now you're lying on the beach or swinging in your hammock or curled up in your big old overstuffed armchair reading the story of my life.

Were you shocked that I had so much to say? I was. And the thoughts keep on coming. The one person who knew I had a lot on my mind because I never shut up was Gail. She's always supported me a thousand percent, no matter what. I'll never forget her reaction when I told her I was writing a book.

"You're *what*?"

"Yep. A chapter book, too. No pictures."

"What's this book about?"

"About two hundred and fifty pages."

I laughed. She didn't. I frowned. She waited.

"It's about me, you, our marriage."

"There's one part I'm worried about."

"Which one?"

"The part about you, me, and our marriage." Then she smiled to let me know she really wasn't that worried. "Just promise me you won't get too personal."

"Aw, honey."

I took both of her hands in mine, looked her in the eye, and said, "Trust me."

To me, the worst thing in the world is shopping for bras with Gail. First of all, she never tells me we're going bra shopping. She knows better. She knows I will not go bra shopping with her on purpose. She has to sneak it by me because I'm too clever for her. She starts out by throwing me a big sweeping curve ball.

"Honey, wanna go to the mall?"

This is a trick question. The moment she asks me, I'm smacking my forehead trying to come up with the right answer. If I say no, there is no chance whatsoever that I will get lucky later. If I say yes, I've compromised my manhood and will end up being dragged from store to store like a pull toy.

"Which mall?"

She smiles coyly. "Westfield."

"Sure."

She got me. She knows that Westfield has two of my favorite stores: Sharper Image and Brookstone. She can be left to run wild while I'll go into Sharper Image and check out their new crazy gadgets, really cool stuff like a pocketknife that shows ESPN. Then I'll go over to Brookstone, where I get into their vibrating massage chair and take a nap. I can't think of a better way to spend an afternoon. I spend so much time in that chair that people believe I come with it, like a footstool.

"I like the chair, but can I get it without Bill?"

"Nope. We'd have to special order one for you. But it's the floor model. I might be able to knock off a few bucks for you. And maybe I can get him to put his boots and socks back on."

When I'm done with my nap and massage, I'll meet Gail at our designated location. By now I'm gone, in some goofy state, oblivious that I've been duped, yet again. I figure we're done shopping. Let's go home, or go out and grab some food. We'll start walking. All of a sudden, Gail will say, "Oh, I just have to run in here for one quick second."

Before I can stop her, she's disappeared into the department store, heading right for the bra section.

Problem number one. There is nothing for a guy to do in the bra section. I can't help Gail pick out a bra. If I say, "Hey, honey, how about this one? This one is *nice*," she'll just glare at me and say, "Bill," and I drop that bra like it's on fire. And once she picks out a bra, I can't go into the dressing room with her and watch her try it on. Much as I'd like to. So I end up standing outside the dressing room in the bra section holding her purse. Once in a while I'll see another guy standing outside a dressing room holding his wife's purse. We'll make eye contact and nod sympathetically, two guys along for the ride, hoping that we'll get lucky later.

While Gail was trying on bras, I started thinking:

Why does a woman even need a new bra? Isn't a bra a lifetime purchase? It's not like jeans that you wear out and scrape up and tear. What are you doing in your bra that wears it out?

I understand regular underwear wearing out. It gets torn being pulled up. But a bra is like Tupperware. It should be indestructible. And as far as lace bras and frilly bras, I don't get the point. It's not like people see 'em. There should be one bra and that's it. Like a universal remote. A universal bra. I think it's all a big consumer scam. My opinion? Whoever invented the bra should be shot publicly.

There might be guys who don't tag along with their wives when they go bra shopping. I just don't know any. The one guy I imagine who doesn't is Chuck Norris. I've seen each one of his movies at least a hundred times. Gail doesn't get how I can watch 'em over and over and never get bored.

"Haven't you already seen this one?"

"Yeah. But this is the best scene, where Chuck leads his old platoon out of Vietnam. He fights a thousand Viet Cong with his bare hands and a can opener."

Chuck Norris never goes to the mall, or grocery shopping. He's too busy kicking people's butts. Still, I bet Chuck's wife called him and said, "Chuck, on your way back getting your platoon out of Vietnam, we're out of fabric softener . . ."

43. CRAPPY PARENT

I might as well get this off my chest.

I'm a crappy parent.

I'm crappy for two major reasons.

One, I'm on the road a lot, sometimes for weeks at a time. So much for the "wait until your father gets home" threat. That doesn't work in our case. Gail can't exactly say, "Just wait until your father gets home—two weeks from Thursday!" Doesn't have quite the same impact.

Fortunately, when it comes to discipline, we got lucky. Emily and Travis are by no means perfect, but they're not problem kids, either. They're kinda like the way I was, God bless 'em. I liked to have fun, but I knew the line between being goofy and a butthole. For the most part, I respected Dad, my mom, and my stepmom and abided by their rules.

I was spanked exactly one time, and that was by a babysitter, an older woman. I don't remember what I did, but I'm sure I deserved it. The weird part was that she spanked me with a flyswatter. Not sure how she came up with that idea, but I can tell you my butt stung like crazy. After that incident, I don't remember seeing her around much.

Discipline doesn't necessarily come as a result of spanking or yelling. It comes from how you're raised. My dad could get me to do what he wanted or to stop doing what I was doing just by giving me a certain look. Some of you may know the look. Some of you may have had dads who gave you the same look. You know that he didn't have to do more than that.

I never knew what the look meant, but I knew this: If I didn't change the way I was acting, something very bad would happen to me. Didn't want that. Did not want to find out what that bad thing was. I had a rich imagination, and I'd seen a lot of movies. I started seeing visions of small windowless cells, belts with spikes, faceless executioners, Chinese water torture . . .

Over the years, I've heard a lot of weird discipline stories from other people. This one stuck with me.

When a friend of mine was fourteen, he mouthed off at his dad. Said a bunch of inappropriate stuff, threatened to punch out the old man. His dad said, "So you think you're a man now, huh? Okay. Let's go to the backyard."

They went to the yard, and the dad said, "Go ahead. I'll let you have the first swing."

My friend swung at him. His dad ducked, then slammed his son in the chest with his open hand. The blow was so hard that my friend thought his chest had caved in. My friend never mouthed off at his dad again.

I could never do that to Travis. I have thought about going into his room, wrestling him away from his Xbox, throwing him on the floor, hogtieing him, and locking him in the closet overnight with just his history book and a flashlight jammed into his mouth. Hey, we all have our fantasies.

Which brings me to the second reason I'm a crappy parent.

I'm a big kid myself.

I had some tough moments in childhood, mainly my parents' divorce, but for the most part I was a happy kid who ran a little wild in college. But I sure had fun. I just want my kids to do better than I did in college, or at least try. Then, I swear, whatever they want to do with their lives, I'm fine with it. If my son wants to be a bartender and play in a rock band, it's all right with me. Long as he's tried his best in school until then. If you're reading this, I mean it, son. Hey, wait, if you're reading this, then you did get something out of your education! All right!

You better get some decent grades. Now, you know I'm not gonna kick your butt. I just told you that.

But listen up.

I will cut you off. I am not lying. I will never reach for my belt. I also won't reach for my wallet.

Want to know the three scariest words in the English language to my son?

Get a job.

I will say this, my kids listen to me because I follow through. That, to me, is the key to discipline. Learned that from Gail. *If you say it, mean it.* The problem with a lot of parents is that they make idle threats.

"Sonny, if you don't stop running around the restaurant, we're going home."

No, you're not. You're not going anywhere. You know it and your kid knows it. You're going to belly up to the buffet and stuff your face and your handbag until the owner calls security, and *then* you're going home. Your kid can hang naked from the light fixture, and you can threaten him all you want. You both know you're staying put until you're done with your meal.

Idle threats don't work. If you threaten to take your kid home if he doesn't shape up, *take the kid home.*

I happened to excel in this one area. If I said I was gonna do something, my kids knew I'd do it. If we were in a restaurant and they were acting up, I just said, "If you don't stop it, we're going home." One time, they didn't stop fooling around; I packed them up, put them in the car, and drove home. Since then, I tell them once, give them the Look, and they shape up. Try it.

It works, I promise you. You can start as early as two. That's when I started with Travis.

We were on a plane, and Travis needed to go to the bathroom. I took him to the head, he did his business, but he wouldn't leave the bathroom. He was fascinated by the way the airplane toilet worked. I don't know what it was. Something about the way the thing flushed. Finally, I'd had enough and I carried him out of the bathroom. He started throwing a fit. He wanted to go back to the bathroom and play with the toilet. I couldn't take it. Plus, he was really bothering all the other passengers. I just leaned in to him and said, "If you don't settle down, I'm gonna take you back to the bathroom, put you in the toilet, and flush you out of the airplane."

Gail glared at me in horror. *"Bill!"*

"What? Look at him. He's quiet, ain't he?"

Told you I was a crappy parent.

I'll say this, Travis didn't act up once the rest of the flight, and to this day he loves to fly.

Although for some reason, he never goes to the bathroom on a plane.

44. HITTING THE CURVE

I t was a few years ago now, on a Saturday night. I'd been on the road and I was wiped out. I just wanted to spend a quiet night at home with Gail. We ordered in food, poured a couple of glasses of wine, and sat in front of the fire, by far my favorite kind of Saturday night.

After a while, we started talking about what it was like when we were kids. Whenever I talk about my childhood, I inevitably get around to the topic of baseball. I could picture myself playing on the diamond in Winslow, hanging out in the dugout, goofing off with the guys on my team. Maybe it was the wine, but a wave of nostalgia came over me, and I suddenly got quiet.

"There's something about baseball," Gail said.

"Yeah. Your team becomes kind of like your family."

Gail nodded. She was a baseball fan herself. She knew the game, and she knew what it meant to me.

"Plus, not to brag, I was pretty good. If I'd decided to pursue baseball instead of comedy—"

She looked at me expectantly, her eyes twinkling. This is how she gets right before she's about to break into hysterical laughter.

"We'd be completely broke," I said.

"Glad you admit it," she said.

I took a sip of wine, then peered at her thoughtfully. "I'm forty-eight. You think it's too late?"

"I think you missed the cutoff by maybe a year," Gail said.

"You're probably right." After a moment I said, "Dreams die hard."

T he envelope arrived two months later. I had no idea what it was, but when I saw that the return address read, "The World Champion Anaheim Angels," I practically ripped it open. Inside was a colorful pamphlet and a detailed letter of instructions addressed to "Bill Engvall, Camper."

"*Welcome to Angels Baseball Fantasy Camp,*" I read.

"Happy birthday," Gail said.

"Whoa," I said, and I couldn't say anything more. I was speechless.

"*For four days you're going to be a Major Leaguer.*"

"Oh myyy. Thank you. This is incredible."

Gail ducked her head shyly and punched me on the arm. I howled, picked her up, and hugged her.

"You like it?"

"Uh *yeah.*" Then I said, more seriously than I'd like to admit: "The

Angels might be looking for a forty-eight-year-old backup shortstop. You never know."

"That's right, Bill," she said. "You never know."

I have been to Heaven.

Heaven is not what you think. There are no pearly gates, no harp music playing, no palm trees swaying.

But there are Angels. Couple dozen of 'em.

They don't have halos or wings or flowing white gowns. Nope. They wear baseball uniforms and batting helmets, and their names are Wright and Fregosi and Kison and DeCinces and Kutcher and Comstock.

Heaven is the 2002 World Champion Angels' locker room. Heaven is the chatter and laughter of men playing a kids' game. Heaven is the crunch of spikes echoing off the concrete clubhouse floor. Heaven is the smell of sweat and Bengay filling the air.

And Heaven is an official Angels' uniform with my name on the back, spelled right, hanging on my very own locker door, also with my name printed on it.

I could've died right then. I'm serious. My life was complete. I didn't even have to go through the camp. You could've taken my picture right then with me in uniform standing next to my locker, and, boom, that would've done it, thank you very much, see ya later, it's been great.

I knew fantasy baseball camp would be fun, but I was unprepared for the sheer joy I felt from the first moment I stepped off the bus that took us to the Angels' spring training facility in Phoenix, Arizona, to the very last instant when I said good-bye to my teammates and coaches. For four full days I had a 24/7 idiot's grin plastered on my face.

It actually started when I got a letter a month earlier detailing all the stuff I should bring and how we should at least attempt to arrive in some semblance of shape. The main thing I was supposed to do, spelled out in big bold letters, was STRETCH.

I don't stretch. First of all, I hate it. Second, I can't.

I sort of tried. Did a couple of lazy knee bends and pulled my arms above my head a few times like I've seen guys do in the on-deck circle. It was useless. I'm about as limber as a lead pipe. I gave up. I figured everybody else at camp would be overweight and out of shape worse than I was. I go to the gym. I work out. I'd be ahead of the game.

Uh, wrong. The first clue that I might have been mistaken was the first day when I put on my uniform and passed by a full-length mirror. I didn't look like a baseball player. I looked like a coach. I looked like Don Zimmer. Only not as buff.

The good news was it wasn't just me. Every fantasy baseball camper strutted past the full-length mirror, checked himself out, and gasped in horror. We were a sorry-looking bunch. A fashion tip: Overweight men should avoid Spandex or any other stretchy-type material. It makes you look gross. I would like to pass a law that any man over the age of forty-five caught wearing a baseball uniform should be arrested. Including managers.

We all looked so ridiculous that it was hard not to laugh. Yet we all loved wearing our uniforms. We were so proud.

After we got our lockers and our uniforms, we went out to the field with our coach, where we worked out and ran laps. Well, a few of us ran. Most of us jogged for about fifty yards until the cramping set in, followed by the limping and the attempts to avoid going into cardiac arrest.

Then we took our positions around the diamond. We shagged fly balls and tried to field grounders. The range of talent and expertise was extreme. Some guys had obviously played ball and took camp seriously. A couple of guys made basket catches in center and showed some range around the horn. Most guys lost cans of corn in the sun and got gobbled up by any grounder hit more than two miles an hour. I was in the middle. I got to the balls I was supposed to. Anything slightly out of my range made me look decrepit.

After fielding, we took batting practice. The coaches watched and, for the most part, refrained from laughing. Every once in a while Jim Fregosi or Rex Hudler would shake his head and jot something on a clipboard. Then we broke for lunch. While we were eating, the coaches held their "draft" and broke us up into four different teams.

After lunch we played our first game. It was a hoot. I played three positions, first base, right field, and third base, which was hysterical because I'm left-handed. Making that throw from third to first was painful. On a shot down the line, I had to pivot like a duck, then set myself, and gun the throw to first. "Gun" might be the wrong word. "Lob" or "dying swan" might be more accurate. What was amazing was that I actually got guys out, because everybody ran so slow.

After the game, we showered, changed, and, like real baseball players, hit the bar. Finally, exhausted, I fell into bed, after setting my alarm for 6:00 A.M. The second day of camp we were going to play a doubleheader.

The alarm clanged at six. I started to lift my head and then realized that I couldn't. I tried to turn over. Nope. Couldn't do that either. Then the pain came over me, and I mean all of me. Every inch. There wasn't a part of me that didn't cry out. I felt like I'd been leveled by a truck. I hurt in places that I had no idea existed within the human body. I didn't know I had a butt muscle. I knew it now. Hurt like hell.

I turned over and I made a noise, a noise I'd never made before. Something between a moan and a prayer. I sat up and I stifled a scream.

Gail looked at me. "Are you all right?"

"I don't think so."

"What's the matter?"

"I hurt. A lot. A real lot."

"Where?"

"Everywhere. Every part of me hurts. I would cry, but my eyelids hurt. The area between my nose and my lip hurts. My hair hurts. Ow, ow, ow."

"Maybe you should rest today. Take a day off."

I stared at her. "What? Are you nuts? I'm not gonna rest! I gotta play ball! I'm a baseball player!"

I somehow climbed to my feet and, with my body scrunched into the shape of a question mark, shuffled into the bathroom. I managed to pull on my uniform and head out toward the bus that would take us to the baseball field.

What a difference a day makes.

Day One of fantasy camp. Guys, eager, excited, hyped up, bounce off the bus, practically run onto the field.

Day Two. Guys are dead. Beyond sore, on the verge of incapacitated. Crawling off the bus, holding on to the side, holding on to each other, moaning, wailing, moving as if they're all part of a geriatric ward, the words "Oh my God" repeated over and over, our anthem.

"Hey, Bill, how you feel?" Hudler and Clyde Wright were watching me hold on to the railing along the perimeter of the ball field.

"Oh my God."

"You sore?"

"Oh. My. *God.*"

Clyde Wright winked at Hudler. "We've got you penciled in to pitch today."

I stopped on a dime. "Really? I haven't pitched since junior high, but I think I can still bring it. Well, if fifty-five counts as bringing it—"

I thought they were going to lose it. "You're not gonna let me pitch, are you?" I said.

Hudler shrugged. "Maybe. Depends if everyone else's arm is dead."

"Okay. Whatever. Excuse me. I have to waddle over to the dugout."

They started laughing again.

"What is so freakin' funny?"

"The way you walk," Hudler said. "You look like a ninety-eight-year-old guy who's crapped in his pants."

"Ha ha. Ow! Oh my God." I turned away and kept walking, trying to pick up my pace. Failing.

Game one was great. It was close and hard fought, and we held on for a win. I played first. At one point, a thin, wiry insurance agent laid a bunt down the first base line. I didn't move. I just stared at it, hoping it would go foul. It hugged the line, stayed fair. I looked at my pitcher and second baseman. "Sorry, I ain't running after it. I mean, I can't. If I bend down, I will be locked into that position for life. When I die, my wife will have to bury me in an L-shaped casket."

My teammates grunted. They understood. I turned to the insurance guy who was standing on first, all puffy-chested and proud. "What the hell are you doing, bunting?"

"We need base runners."

"That's cheap. You know none of us can run. Or bend over."

He shrugged. "I play to win."

"Dude, this ain't the World Series. It's fantasy camp." I glowered at him. "Are you gonna try to steal? Because if you are, I'll save you the trouble and spike you right now."

Game two was another back-and-forth affair. About midway through, our manager, Rex Hudler, called a conference on the mound. This in itself was totally cool. Always wanted to be part of a conference on the mound. We were all huddled together, and I pictured myself on ESPN.

Rex looked at our pitcher. "Your arm is dead," he said.

The pitcher, a sixty-eight-year-old used-car salesman whose toupee kept falling off during his windup, said, "You know it. I got nothing left."

"No offense," Rex said. "You had nothing before."

Rex took off his cap and scratched the back of his neck with the bill. "Engvall, how's your arm?"

"Feels like an overcooked piece of spaghetti."

"That's better than anyone else. You're pitching." He plopped the ball into the pocket of my mitt. "Don't hurt yourself. Well, don't hurt yourself any worse."

I took a deep breath, both to calm my nerves and to try to erase the grin that had now attacked my face. I must've looked like a smiley-face sticker.

"Runners on first and second," Eli, the fifty-three-year-old short-stop and school principal, reminded us. "Let's turn two."

Rex stifled a laugh, then turned a deep purple as he tried to hold back hysterics. "Let's turn *two?* That's our strategy? We haven't turned two all week. We can barely turn one."

"I ain't gonna be striking anyone out," I said. "I hope we can turn two."

"Just let 'em hit it to us. We got your back," Eli said, and swatted me on my butt, which I found unnecessary and kind of disturbing.

Turned out I was wrong. I struck out the first batter I faced on three pitches. Brick, a fifty-seven-year-old investment banker, had obviously never seen pitching that slow. After swinging and missing twice, he stepped out of the box and pleaded: "Can you throw it any faster?"

"I don't think so. I'll try."

I grunted like Monica Seles serving and threw him my heater. Brick swung hard, about five minutes early, and nearly screwed himself into the ground.

"Sorry," I said.

"I think I threw my back out," he said.

We eventually lost that game when Eli, attempting to field a text-book two-hopper, allowed the ball to skitter though his legs as if they were croquet wickets. Our left fielder, a sixty-three-year-old travel agent, fortunately was backing Eli up. Unfortunately, he threw the ball over the first baseman's head, into the stands. Two runs scored. Ball game.

It didn't matter. We split the doubleheader, and despite our injuries and inept baseball playing, we remained, for these four days, Angels.

They saved the best for last.

The final day of camp, we got to play a game against the former Angels. Campers against coaches. I got to hit against real Major Leaguers. A dream come true. Countless times I'd sat in front of the TV, watching a ball game, and wondered: *Could I ever hit that pitching? Is it really that fast? Is it really impossible to hit a Major League curveball?*

The answers are nope, yep, and *duhhh.*

The day of the big game, I fielded grounders at first and squinted into the crowd. There were maybe two dozen people, all family and friends, including Gail, who sat in the stands cradling her digital camera. We made eye contact and she waved. I tipped my cap, cool as a Major Leaguer. Inside I was bursting. I kicked at the dirt, then jogged into the dugout to get ready to hit.

In the second inning, I stepped into the batter's box and found myself facing Keith Comstock, who, in addition to being a former big leaguer who hurled for the Angels and was currently an Angels minor league pitching coach, is left-handed. I, too, am left-handed. Advantage him. Teams typically bring in southpaws to face tough left-handed batters because it's hard for lefty hitters to pick up the ball.

Yeah. I'm sure that's why the Angels went to Keith to face me. Had to be the fear factor.

I dug in.

Keith went into his windup and delivered his out pitch, his curve.

The ball came straight at me, then all of a sudden dipped and dived into the dirt as if it were falling off a table. I swung and came up empty. Nothing but air. I'd say, conservatively, that I'd missed it by three feet.

"Okay, now throw me your curve," I said.

Keith laughed. "Think I'll bring the cheese."

He reared back and threw a fastball, which just missed the outside corner. Or so I was told, since I never saw it.

"Pretty obvious you're afraid of me, dude," I said, pointing the bat toward the right field seats.

Keith pounded the ball into his glove. I took a deep breath. He went into his delivery, and . . . here it came again. The curve. The hook. Uncle Charley. The deadliest pitch in baseball.

I held back a half second, then swung, allowing for the break this time.

I never saw the ball hit the bat.

But I heard it.

That sound. The sweetest sound in sports. The whoosh of the bat connecting with the hard rubber of the ball, and then *CRACK—*

A sharp grounder to short. I sprinted out of the box, head down, stunned that I'd hit a Major League curve, determined to beat it out. The shortstop scooped the ball up and lasered a throw to first. I was out by ten feet.

I felt as if I'd hit a walk-off home run. I raised both arms in triumph.

I'd hit the curve.

Okay, it was an out, but I hit it. Got good wood on it, too.

Now I had to be cool.

I trotted across the diamond, head held high, barely able to contain my smile.

"Engvall."

Keith. He was grinning back at me. Grinning with pride. He pulled off his glove and tossed it to me. "It's yours, man. You hit my curve."

Cradling Keith's glove against my chest, I broke into a run, and kept running into our dugout, where I was mobbed by my team.

"Nice hit," Rex Hudler said, tussling up my hair.

"I never saw it," I admitted.

Hud shrugged. "You hit it. Hit a Major League curveball."

"Yeah," I said. "I hit the curve."

But it hadn't sunk in.

Still hasn't.

45. SEÑOR A-HOLAY

I'm such a guy.

I'm such a guy that all Gail has to do is give me a little bit of rope and I will happily hang myself.

Exhibit A. A couple years ago, Angels Clyde Wright and Keith Comstock, who had become close friends, invited Gail and me to join them at the stadium bar before Opening Day for an informal camp reunion. We started reminiscing about camp.

"Speaking of which," Keith said, "did you know that the gift shop downstairs sells official Rawlings bats for sixty bucks and they'll laser your name right in the barrel?"

"No," I said. "Are you kidding me?"

"I kid you not."

"Sixty bucks? I'm going there right now and get me one of those."

I drained my beer and started to head out. Gail grabbed my wrist in a vise-like grip, stopping me cold. She works out and for some reason has developed superhuman strength in her fingers. When she grabs you, it's like the Jaws of Life.

"Bill." She squeezed a little harder.

"Uh, yeah?" The blood was starting to drain out of my face.

"Maybe you should get one of those bats for Father's Day. Or your birthday. That might be, you know, *better*."

"Better than what? I want the bat now. It's Opening Day."

She pinched my wrist harder. "Bill."

"Owww. What?"

"Don't get the bat now. You don't need it this minute."

Somehow I managed to pull my wrist away. "Yes. I do. I need it now. I want it now."

Now. I'm a guy. Therefore, I am thick. So this is what was going through my mind:

She's unbelievable. She is busting my chops over a sixty-dollar bat? I don't blink an eye if she buys jewelry. I don't say a word if she goes shopping and buys another ten pairs of shoes. It wasn't necessary for me to buy her a new car, but I did anyway. Why? Because I wanted to. Because she deserved it. And now she's giving me grief over a SIXTY-DOLLAR BASEBALL BAT??

"Bill, honey, why don't you have another beer?"

"Gee, Gail, they cost six dollars. Are you sure we can afford it? That's an awful lot to pay for a beer. I'll just get a glass of water and finish up these beer nuts. I'll be fine. You're right. It's stupid to spend sixty bucks on an official Rawlings baseball bat with my name engraved in it. We could put that sixty bucks toward college or something more practical like a lube job for your new car—"

Yeah, I was relentless. Bless her, Gail didn't say a word. She just nursed her beer and let me babble on, guy that I am, idiot that I was.

Because what I didn't know was that she and Clyde Wright had already gotten me the bat, which they presented to me during the seventh inning stretch.

It had been lovingly engraved with the nickname the guys had given me in camp and that I had more than earned in the bar with Gail.

The bat said: BILL "A-HOLE" ENGVALL.

I t didn't stop there.

At the time Comstock was the pitching coach for the minor league Rancho Cucamonga Angels. During the season, he invited me to come down to the stadium and work out with the team before a game. I was totally jazzed about it, but I hesitated, didn't want to step on anyone's toes.

"You sure these kids won't mind?"

"Nah. I asked them. They'd love it."

From fantasy camp to shagging balls with minor league prospects. What could be better?

One night, I threw on my sweats, got in my truck, and trekked an hour or so from my house to a dusty minor league field to play baseball with future Major Leaguers. When I got there, Keith brought me into the bullpen and we tossed the ball around. Then I shagged balls for the team while they took batting practice. I don't think there was a player on the team older than twenty-two, and most were shy Latin kids, who were chasing the American Dream. I loved 'em.

That first night, after working out with the team, I sat in the dugout next to Keith and cheered them on. This was even better than fantasy camp. This was real.

Guess the team didn't mind me hanging around, because they invited me back the next night. And the next. Before I knew it I'd spent two straight weeks playing catch with Keith in the bullpen and shagging flies during BP. Then one day Keith called me into his office before practice.

"We got a situation," he said.

"What's the problem?"

"A lot of the fans show up early to watch BP. They've been asking who the guy is who's not in uniform."

"Oh, I see. Hey, Keith, it's cool. I don't want to cause any trouble."

"No worries. You just gotta wear a uniform is all. Tell you what. Grab one out of the locker over there."

"Really?"

"Yeah. Take that first one."

I practically shot over to the locker. I guess to people like Keith who've been around baseball their whole lives, this was no big deal, but I was like a little kid. I whipped open the locker and started putting on an official Rancho Cucamonga Angels uniform. I hauled up the pants.

"Wow. These fit pretty good. This guy must've been my size."

Keith shrugged and sipped his coffee. He was too busy going over the stat sheet from last night's game to pay any attention to me. I put on the socks, then laced up my cleats. Then I grabbed the jersey, flipped it over, and read what was stenciled on the back:

13. A-Hole.

It must've been the look I gave Keith, because he spit out his coffee and started gasping with laughter. Finally, he managed to choke out: "So it fits, huh?"

"Yeah," I said. "So does the uniform."

I wore my uniform proudly. Wore it for a week without incident until one of the players came over to me while I was tossing the ball in the bullpen with Keith. He was holding back a smirk. He was a young Mexican kid who was trying to develop a curve to go along with his 95 mph fastball.

"My mom's here," he said. "She wants to know if you're Puerto Rican."

"She can't see that I'm a forty-eight-year-old white guy?"

"The name on your back," he said. "She thinks your name is Aholay."

Now Keith started to lose it.

"Tell her she's right," I said. "I'm Puerto Rican. My name is Javier Aholay."

The kid nodded and jogged away.

The mom must've spread the word, because before the next few games I heard people in the stands shouting for me during warm-ups: "Nice catch, Aholay!" "Good throw, Aholay!" "Hey, Aholay, you trying to make Web Gems?"

Then someone changed the pronunciation.

I was sitting in the dugout with Keith between innings, and an eight-year-old kid poked his head in. "Excuse me. Could I have a baseball?"

"Sure, kid," I said, and tossed him a practice ball.

"Thanks, Mr. A-Hole," he said.

Keith and I both burst out laughing after the kid ran away. He was back, after the game, waiting for me as I filed off the field in the midst of the players.

"Excuse me again, Mr. A-Hole," the kid said, offering me the baseball I'd given him. "Would you sign it?"

"Sure," I said, and Keith handed me a pen. As I thought about what to write, I saw the kid looking at me with big saucer eyes. It occurred to me then how important this was to him. He was just a kid, his whole life ahead of him, and I was this larger-than-life figure, this icon. I meant something to him, the way that John Wayne or my granddad or my dad meant something to me. I had to write something meaningful, words of wisdom that he could hang on to forever, something that he could someday show his wife, his kids, his grandkids, with pride.

Got it.

I scribbled my message onto his baseball.

Don't be an A-Hole.

46. THE INVISIBLE MAN

Whenever anyone asks why baseball is so important to me, I use a line from George Carlin.

"Because the object of the game is to come home," I say.

In the end, that's what life is all about: coming home.

I love performing, but when I'm on the road, what keeps me going is that I know I'm coming home.

Of course, home is not my house. Home is my family. And home is being who I really am. As you've seen, who I am at home is not that far from who I am in my act. I really am just a guy.

But the older I get, the more I find that something bizarre is happening to me.

I'm becoming invisible.

Maybe that's part of being an older guy. I know this. I hear myself saying stuff, and nobody in the family answers me. I know I'm talking. I hear the words echoing in my head. But nobody acknowledges me.

Like I'll tell Travis to feed the dogs. When I get home, the dogs are whimpering, scratching at their bowls, looking at me like they've been living in a gulag for the last few hours.

"Travis, did you feed the dogs?"

"Uh, no. Was I supposed to?"

"I told you to."

"You did? Sorry. I never heard that."

I know that half of that is his being a guy and not hearing anything that doesn't involve eating, sleeping, and, because he's in the ninth grade, video games. The other half is that I'm invisible.

I'll be driving somewhere with Gail and I'll remind her of something I told her.

"You never told me that."

"Yes, I did. Told you that yesterday."

"No, you didn't. I would've remembered."

That's my cue to shut up. I may be invisible, but I'm not an idiot. There is no winning this fight. Then, even though I know I told her, I find myself thinking: *Huh. Maybe I didn't tell her.*

My becoming invisible is happening more and more. Or maybe I'm just starting to notice it more.

I was in the bank the other day, waiting in line. The teller said, "Next," and waved to the guy behind me.

I said, "What about me?"

"Sorry," the teller said. "I didn't see you."

"I've been standing right here."

When I finally got to the window, before she could complete my transaction, the teller said, "Could I see some ID?"

"I've been banking here for two years. I come here every Wednesday. You waited on me last Wednesday. Didn't ask me for ID last week, or the week before, or the week before that. Why do you need it this week?"

She shrugged. "I don't recognize you."

I've decided that being invisible is part of being a guy, especially a guy who's around the family a lot. You become kind of like furniture or a large plant in the corner. You're pretty much looked at the way most people look at tires on a car. Nobody ever walks up to a car and says, first thing, "Those are nice tires."

That's the way people look at most guys.

Yeah, I noticed him. I think. He didn't stand out in any way. His head didn't seem too big. His ears didn't hang down to his waist. He seemed fine.

I've even become invisible on the road, right after I'm done performing.

I once finished doing my set and went into a nearby restaurant for a bite to eat. A couple of people noticed me and asked for autographs. I finished signing for them, and a woman came up to me, looked me right in the eye, and said, "No, it ain't him."

I first noticed I was becoming invisible a few years ago when my daughter, Emily, was sixteen. I'd be home, I'd speak, and nobody would answer me. At first I wasn't sure I wasn't talking out loud, but then I was pretty sure I was, since the dogs' ears seemed to stick up when I'd talk to them.

It seemed I was invisible most often when I wanted something. I would speak and . . . nothing. I'd repeat it. Still nothing. I'd wave my hand in front of my family's faces. They wouldn't blink. I'd talk, and my voice didn't seem to cause a ripple in the room.

"I'm starving. Let's order a pizza."

Silence.

"Okay. How about Mexican?"

No response.

"Chinese? Japanese? Korean? A box of Chiclets? Hello? I know you're out there, I can see you ignoring me. Fine. I don't have to order any food. I'll just sit in the corner and gnaw on my own foot."

But if they wanted something, miraculously, they'd see me.

"Daddy?"

"Yes, Emily?"

"I love you."

"Love you, too, Em."

"I missed you so much at school today. You should text me. By the way, I saw the cutest cashmere sweater in Bloomingdale's. My birthday's in a few months, so would you buy it for me? And guess what? You're in luck. It's on sale, marked down to four hundred dollars."

For a four-hundred-dollar sweater, she could see me clear as day, but if I want to order a ten-dollar pizza, I'm invisible.

I'm not really complaining about being invisible. As I said before, I think it's just part of being a guy. Actually, I know that becoming invisible is what lies ahead for most people in show business. Sad but true.

Nothing lasts forever. I'm riding high now, reached the peak of the roller coaster, but at any moment I can start that steep, torrid, heart-stopping decline. I could hit a loop and head on up again, you never know. Or the ride could stop and the attendant, or, as I call him, the President of Show Business, might take me off.

When that happens, I'll be fine. Don't know where we'll be. Maybe in Dallas. Or on our ranch. Or even back in Winslow. You never know.

Being just a guy, I can only see five minutes in front of me. Gail can see the future. Or at least she tries to prepare for what's ahead. I'm too in the moment. I could be outside mowing the lawn and if my buddies drove by and said, "Hey, Bill, we're going to Vegas. You in?" chances are I'd say, "Hell, yes," drop the mower, and get in the car. I can't help it. I'm a *guy*.

I just know that someday, when everybody does forget my name, when I'm the answer to a trivia question—*Who was the fourth guy on the Blue Collar Comedy Tour?*—when I really do become invisible, I want to sit on a front porch somewhere with Gail, hold her hand, and say, "It was pretty fun, wasn't it?"